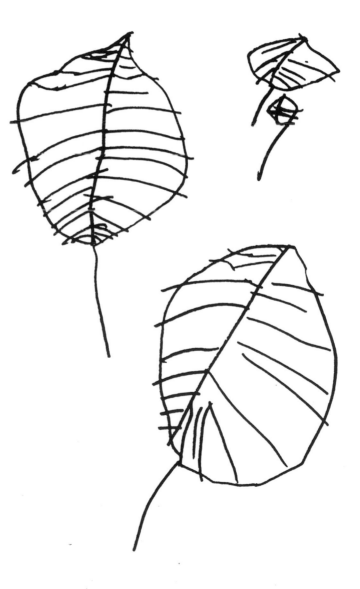

Second Edition 2007, reprinted 2009, 2015
First Edition 2001, reprinted 2002 & 2004

Peppinot Press
PO Box 1775, Byron Bay NSW 2481, Australia
Web: www. peppinotpress.com.au

National Library of Australia Cataloguing-in-Publication Data:
        Kolbe, Ursula.
         Rapunzel's supermarket : all about young children and their art.

        2nd ed.
        Bibliography.
        ISBN 9780975772218.
        ISBN 0 9757722 1 X.

        1. Children's art. 2. Child artists. I. Title.
        704.083

Every effort has been made to clear permissions for the poems, artworks and photographs in this book.
However, in the event of any oversight, the publishers apologise and guarantee to make the due
acknowledgement or amendment in a subsequent reprint. The publishers would like to thank the artists,
poets, galleries and agencies for their kind permission to reproduce the following works.

Dürer, Albrecht: *Young Hare*. Reproduced by permission of Albertina, Wien.
Copyright © in the remaining illustrated artworks remains with the artists. Reproduced by permission
of Kate Dorrough, Sophie Gralton, Geoff Harvey, Audrey Rhoda, Guan Wei, Dhukal Wirrpanda,
Galuma Maymuru, Edna Mariong Watson and Patricia Karbo Jarvis.

Bell, Anne: 'Mushrooming' published in *School Magazine* (NSW Department of Education). Permission:
Anne Bell. Boult, Jenny: 'tree'. Permission: Christine Boult. de la Mare, Walter: 'Silver' from *Complete Poems of
Walter de la Mare*, 1969. Permission: The Literary Trustees of Walter de la Mare and the Society of Authors
as their representative. de Regniers, Beatrice Schenk: 'If You Find A Little Feather' from *Something Special* by
Beatrice Schenk de Regniers Copyright © 1958, 1986 Beatrice Schenk de Regniers. Permission: Marian
Reiner. Livingston, Myra Cohn: 'Fletcher Avenue' from *Worlds I Know and Other Poems* by Myra Cohn
Livingston. Copyright ©1985 Myra Cohn Livingston. Permission: Marian Reiner. Oodgeroo of the tribe
Noonuccal (formerly known as Kath Walker): 'Corroboreei' from *My People*, third edition, Jacarandah Press,
1990. Permission: John Wiley & Sons Australia. Reeves, James: 'Animals' Houses' from © James Reeves,
Complete Poems For Children (Heineman). Reprinted by permission of the James Reeves Estate.

Excerpt from *Peaks and Valleys: An Autobiography* by Lloyd Rees. Copyright ©1985 Lloyd Rees.
Permission: Harper Collins Publishers. Excerpt from *The Poetics of Space* by Gaston Bachelard. (Tr. Maria
Holos) Copyright © 1969. Permission: Penguin Putnam.Excerpts from *Chambers for a Memory Palace* by
Donlyn Lyndon and Charles W. Moore. Copyright © 1994. Permission: The MIT Press.

Photography by Ursula Kolbe except: Wendy Arnold (author pic), Jason Cresswell (p 113), Jennifer Eaton (pp.
49 a, 104 a-b); Sandy Edwards (pp. 7, 8, 11, 13 a-b, 23 a, 40, 69 a-b, 71 a-b, 72 b, 73, 81, 105 a-c, 106 a-b, 115, 121
a-c)Peter Endersbee (pp. 25 a-c, 65, 80, 92); Anne Evans (p. 49 bottom); Karin Kolbe (pp. 29 bottom, 31 a, 124);
Kirsty Liljegren (p. 58 a); Beulah von Rensberg (pp 51).

Original text design by rat:o
Cover and 2nd edn update/additions by Melanie Feddersen, i2iDesign
Set in FF Scala & FF Scala Sans
Printed in China at Everbest Printing Co

Notice to the Reader
All care has been taken in the preparation of the information herein, but no responsibility can be accepted
by the publishers or author for any damages, mishaps or accidents resulting from the misinterpretation of this
work. The reader is expressly warned to adopt all safety precautions that might be indicated by the activities
herein and to avoid all potential hazards.

Rapunzel's Supermarket

All about young children and their art

Second Edition

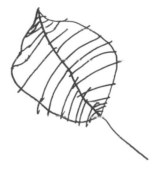

URSULA KOLBE

Peppinot Press

Preface to the Second Edition

I never dreamt when *Rapunzel's Supermarket* was first published in July 2001 that it would reach so many readers, and even become a textbook internationally. Now, five years later, it seems time to produce a second edition. I do so not out of need to change the original content (as this is still valid) nor to add new material within the body of the original. That would throw the careful interweaving of text and pictures out of kilter and make the book cumbersome. However, I do wish to revisit the original in the light of recent publications in early education, as well as world events that seem to impact more and more on children's lives – all of which make it necessary to expand the reading list. Moreover, since writing *It's Not a Bird Yet: The Drama of Drawing*, and listening to teachers and parents during the past five years, I have gained fresh insights about points I should re-emphasise. These, then, are reflected in a brief new section 'Sunlight and Shadow' at the end of this book.

My thanks go to all who so generously shared with me observations, thoughts and visions since *Rapunzel* was first published. Special thanks go to Wendy Shepherd and Laurie Kocher for their valuable comments on the manuscript for this edition.

U. Kolbe, September 2006

ALSO BY URSULA KOLBE

It's Not a Bird Yet: The Drama of Drawing
(Peppinot Press, 2005)

Clay & Children: More Than Making Pots
(Early Childhood Australia, 1997)

Drawing and Painting With Under-Threes, with Jane Smyth
(Early Childhood Australia, 2000)

Contents

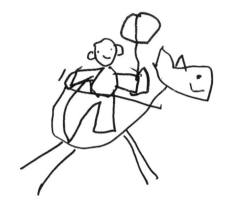

To the memory of my parents
ILSE and HENDRIK JAN ZUIDEMA

THE STORY BEHIND THE TITLE

'Rapunzel's Supermarket' is the name four young children once gave to a structure they had made out of clay. (Rapunzel is a Brothers Grimm fairy tale character.) The structure itself did not last long – in fact, only a morning. But that didn't matter. What mattered was the children's deep involvement and the skills they contributed as they tried, over an hour, various ways to save the building from collapse. Above all, what mattered were the ideas they shared while creating an invented world that was partly 'real' and partly imaginary.

While this book contains many examples of pieces of work that did last and are valuable records of children's thoughts and feelings, 'Rapunzel's Supermarket' reminds us of the importance of 'the doing' and how this also deserves our full attention. Each experience with materials is valuable, and each is a stepping stone to other pieces of work.

About This Book

Years ago I accepted a job I thought would only be temporary, working as an artist with young children in an innovative early learning centre. It was an experience that opened my eyes to the world of early childhood education – a world I have never since left. Rather, I have gone on marvelling at the wealth of knowledge we can uncover about how children learn. This book brings together many of my discoveries about children as powerful image-makers.

The book is intended for all who live and work with children from infancy to six years, and is as much for families as for staff in early childhood programs. In suggesting how you can help children realise their potential as image-makers, it is both a practical guide to children's early image-making and a celebration of what they can do. I hope it reveals how visual arts experiences can be food for thought and the imagination, and a source of joy and wellbeing in children's lives.

EAGER EXPLORERS

At the heart of the book is a vision of children as eager explorers – explorers with an intense desire and will to make sense of their world. Some of the most effective means they have for explaining things to themselves are drawing, painting and claywork. While using them to make images, they explore feelings and ideas, and through their images they communicate thoughts to others as well as themselves.

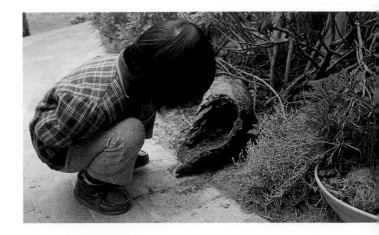

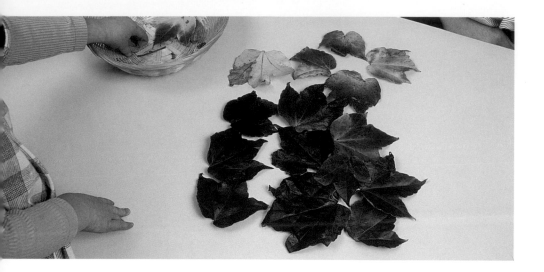

LEARNING TO SEE

'Learning to see' is another theme in this book. Being attentive to things, seeing familiar things anew, seeing the extraordinary in the ordinary are aspects of this theme which recur throughout. Why? Because 'learning to see' – with all the senses – is the starting point for learning about the world, the starting point for making images.

While writing this book and talking to families about it, I found 'learning to see' was a theme that appealed to many. The more I talked about the pleasures of looking at the world with children, the more people began telling me stories – about the magic of taking their five-month-old to see the sights at a fruit market, about taking time to watch their two- and three-year-old painstakingly arrange leaves for a caterpillar's 'dinner', about seeing a six-year-old's delight in opening a flower press. The book celebrates these shared moments.

HOW TO USE THIS BOOK

The book is not meant to be read from beginning to end. Dip into it at random if searching for ideas, or turn to the table of contents and index for specific information. Whatever your starting point, I hope you will find in its pages a rich mosaic of images, ideas and poetry to enchant the eye and feed the imagination.

Drawing, painting, claywork, collage and construction feature prominently, but there are also glimpses of other kinds of image-making. Children use all sorts of materials – not just 'art' materials – to represent things, to express and communicate ideas and feelings. I'm thinking of the buildings they make with toy blocks, for instance, or the miniature worlds they create with leaves and twigs, or the ways they use dress-ups to transform themselves. Such examples, I feel, also belong in this book.

Each chapter offers suggestions for ways you can support, guide and also challenge children. Some suggestions apply particularly to children in group settings, while others may be more relevant to families at home. I hope the pictures and stories included will help you as much as they have helped me in learning to look at what children do and observe things from their point of view.

Children vary greatly. Each child has unique qualities and a unique style, so choose suggestions from the book to suit individual strengths, interests, abilities and physical requirements.

To help you follow intersecting threads, each section ends with a list of related areas. This means, for example, that while key information on drawing appears in the Drawing section, you will also be directed to other sections that relate to drawing.

I have chosen some reproductions of works of art to give inspiration and enjoyment to children as much as to adults. Children, after all, like looking at 'grown-up' books. On my parents' bookshelves were two art books: one on the German artist, Dürer, and one on the Dutch artist, Rembrandt. Although I can't say that as a child I particularly liked any of the images in them, except Dürer's *Young Hare*, I certainly remember poring over them because they fascinated me.

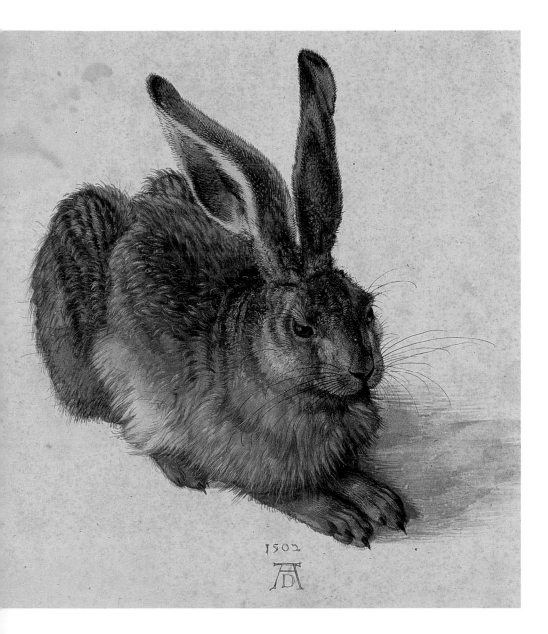

I've loved this watercolour since childhood. The hare squats calmly, yet is also attentive and alert. I suppose it's Dürer's deep respect for this gentle animal – reflected in every brushstroke, each faithfully recorded detail – that makes it such a marvellous portrayal.

Albrecht Dürer (German, 1471 - 1528)
Young Hare, 1502
Watercolour, 25.1 x 22.6 cm
Albertina, Wien

The warmth of your presence *in itself* gives support. It sustains children as they interact with the world around them. It encourages them as they play with materials and create images.

A wordless dialogue of exchanged glances and smiles can often be enough. On other occasions children are eager for guidance or additional challenges. However, don't feel you need special skills to provide them.

The key to developing confidence in working with children begins with watching. Take time to watch. Observe children's absorbed attention, their total concentration, their sheer delight as they play with colours and shapes. Watch their gestures and facial expressions. Listen to their words. Appreciate what they do.

Most importantly, give children time – time to look and ponder, time to explore materials, time to repeat things over and over again. And offer materials and tools of the best quality you can afford, materials that let children shape their own ideas and enable them to realise their potential as image-makers and knowledge-builders.

While I have included the ages of children in many examples as a guide, this is not meant to suggest that all children of similar ages will do or say similar things. As I have already said, children vary enormously. It is unfair and unhelpful to compare them. This applies to all children, but particularly to those with special needs. We need to notice and appreciate each individual's strengths and abilities, each child's special personality.

Magic in Everyday Things

MUSHROOMING

I went mushrooming over the hill
On a morning clear as thrushes' song.
I brought my bucket back empty
But my five senses were filled to the brim
By the overflowing day.

ANNE BELL

The sense of wonder that we are all born with – a sensitivity to the look and feel and sounds of things – matters a great deal.

If we try to look at things *with* children, if we value the moments when they stop and stare and wonder at the world, then we probably do more for their creative, aesthetic and artistic development than a host of specific art activities might ever do.

Busy parents and professionals working with babies and toddlers sometimes tell me they feel they don't do enough 'art' with the children. But the visual arts are not only about making things with materials: they begin with looking and touching. Sometimes we simply need to slow down and look intently at things with children – movements of creatures, the gleam of colours in a shell or in grains of sand trickling through fingers, a favourite picture book.

Time to stop and stare, to touch and listen, time to explore and make choices, and time just to *be*, is essential. A heightened sense of awareness may grow slowly or it might come in a flash. But unhurried and unstructured time to perceive things – through all the senses – is vital if we are to find magic and mystery in things with children.

Looking at things with children is a two-way street: just as you point out things worth noticing, they show you things you've missed. And sometimes just observing things silently together is enough.

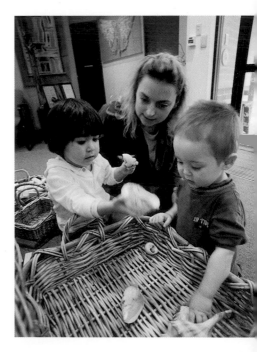

Time for Looking

The more we see, touch, hear, smell and taste, the more we discover and learn about the world. Feeding the senses helps our minds to develop. When do these experiences start?

From the moment of birth infants are intent on responding and exploring. In learning to respond to their surroundings – the sights and sounds, the textures, tastes and smells – they lay foundations for later learning. When they have such sensory experiences in the presence of a loving person it seems that important faculties of their minds take root. Interaction with another is crucial.

PRICKLY PINEAPPLES AND HAIRY COCONUTS

Here is a wonderful example of the kind of gift parents spontaneously give their children when they share the delights of the everyday world – an example of how ordinary things matter.

The baby's father made a lovely comment: 'Our trip to the fruit market is the highlight of his week. Lachlan just loves touching all the different textures – the prickly pineapples, the hairy coconuts, the smooth watermelons, and all the different smells ... he can't have enough of it!'

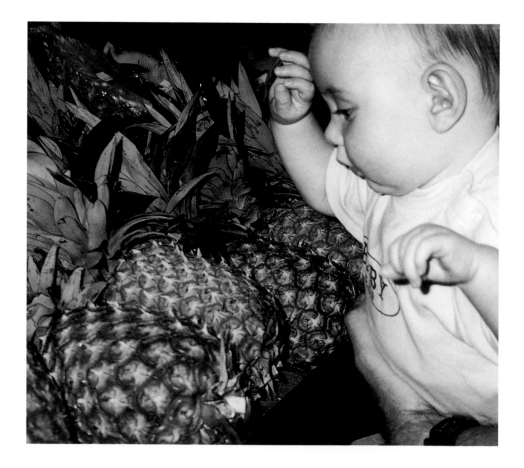

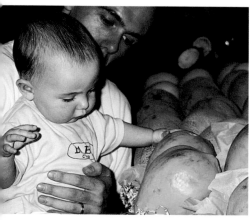

Everyday sights become extraordinary if you take time to watch. For instance, soon after Oscar, my godson, was born, his mother would sit with him on the curb of a quiet street to watch pigeons. From Oscar's ringside seat, the wheeling, fluttering mass of creatures flying down to feed on breadcrumbs was spellbinding. As months passed, watching pigeons became a calming ritual for both mother and child, a special time.

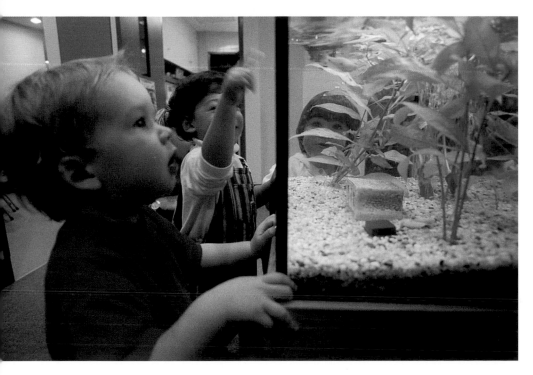

Pausing to watch the centre's goldfish every day after lunch is a little ritual that a small group of very young toddlers have invented for themselves.

Not just any spoons, but beautiful spoons, intriguing spoons, spoons for different purposes, spoons of wood, metal and plastic, and in all sorts of shapes.

BEAUTIFUL SPOONS

Spoons are very ordinary objects. However, as I watched two-year-olds place spoons in a basket and then back on a cloth with such delight and seriousness, I realised that spoons can also be special. In this example, the spoons ask to be sorted and re-sorted, grouped and regrouped.

I DIDN'T KNOW YOU HAD A GOLD ONE!

You can expose children to the world of art in many ways.

While works of art may not be 'everyday' things, art in the form of inexpensive reproductions and hand-crafted objects can become part of children's everyday world. For example, you might display postcard reproductions at child height anywhere – on walls, on sides of cupboards, above the bathroom basin.

Children are observant. They often notice far more than we suppose. In one playroom where I taught, we had an Indonesian puppet with silver trimmings on a display shelf. As it was fragile, we eventually replaced it with another very like the first – except that the new puppet had gold trimmings. The next morning four-year-old Mick, whom we had never seen even look at the original puppet, immediately said: 'I didn't know you had a gold one!'

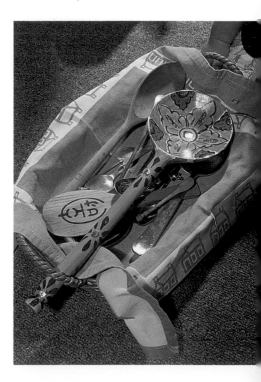

This is for you! You often hear these words from children as they thrust into your hand something they've made or found. Some linger long enough to watch your reaction, others scuttle away immediately, comforted or reassured perhaps with the sense of having left you with a little bit of themselves. It seems to support their bond with you. For a gift is a gift of the self, not simply an object.

Transforming something into a gift makes it special, a treasure. To my mind this invites a different way of seeing, or maybe even a chance to see the object properly for the first time.

IF YOU FIND A LITTLE FEATHER

If you find a little feather,
a little white feather,
a soft and tickly feather,
*   it's for you.*

A feather is a letter
from a bird,
and it says,
'Think of me.
Do not forget me.
Remember me always.
Remember me forever.
Or remember me
at least
until
the little feather
is
lost.'

So ...

... if you find a little feather
a little white feather,
a soft and tickly feather,
*   it's for you.*
*   Pick it up*
*   and ...*
*   put it in your pocket!*

BEATRICE SCHENK DE REGNIERS

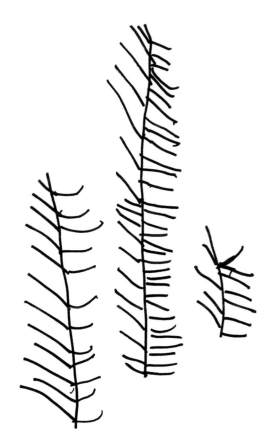

'Feathers' by a four-year-old,
drawn after she had handled
and talked about feathers
for several minutes with other
children. While drawing,
she frequently stopped to look
at the feathers again.

The remaining sections in this chapter focus on discoveries children make as they respond to the look and feel of things and play with colours and shapes. These are the sorts of discoveries that excite image-makers, both young and old. And they become special when shared with another.

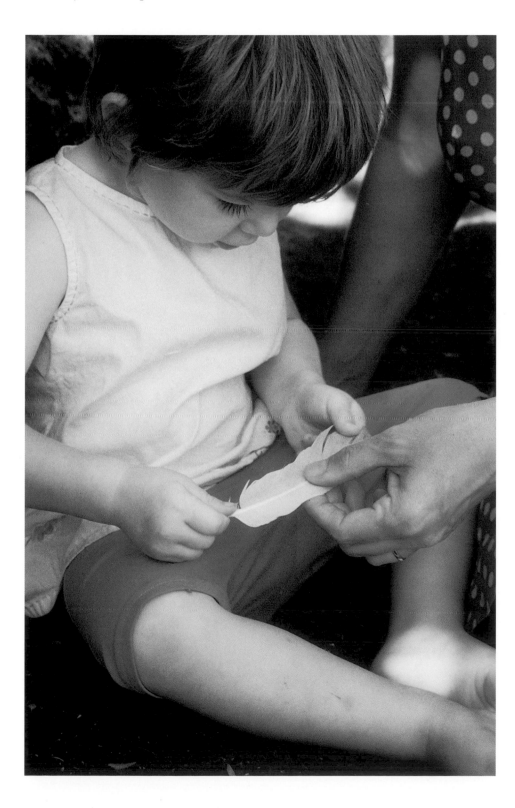

Looking at Marks and Lines

'Snail,' says Chris (23 months) in response to a spiralling line appearing at the end of his paint brush. 'I'm making water, lots of water, it's a river!' says Sally (3 years 2 months) as she makes an ever-deepening mass of rhythmically swirling lines with a pen. 'He's jumping, jumping!' says three-year-old Vicky as she makes a row of zigzags depicting a leaping horse.

This is more than simply 'doing and making'. There is a constant give and take between the children and what is happening on the paper, a circuit between eye, mind and hand.

It starts with the joy of making marks and lines. Gradually lines begin to 'speak' to the imagination. Children become aware that lines can represent things – not only people and objects, but also movements and even sounds.

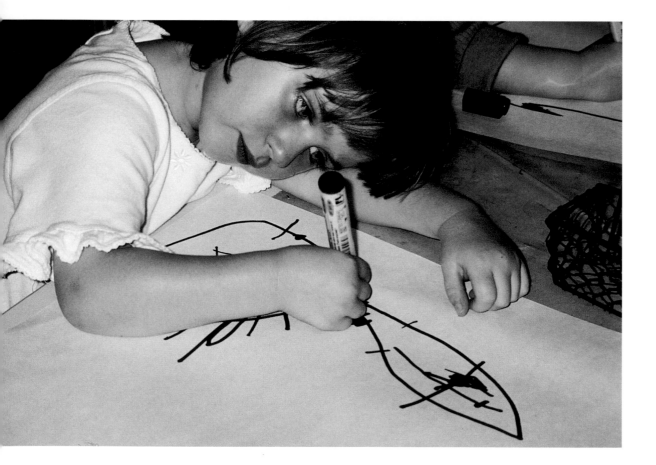

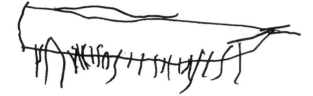

BOLD AND THICK, FINE AND SPIDERY

Lines are the bare bones of a drawing. Bold and thick, or fine and spidery, swirling and spiralling, or sharp and jagged, lines can vary enormously.

As each tool has its unique way of making a line, so each child uses lines in his or her own way. A child's personal rhythm is embedded in every line of a drawing or painting.

As children become experienced drawers, they begin to make certain kinds of lines intentionally.

FIERCE TEETH

'This dinosaur's got fierce teeth,' announces Tom (4 years 11 months), grinning wickedly as he shows me his drawing. 'These other ones don't have fierce teeth, but he's got fierce teeth, very fierce.'

Indeed they are fierce. While words like 'spiky', 'jagged', 'sharp', 'piercing', and 'pointed' are not part of Tom's *verbal* vocabulary, it seems from his drawings that they are definitely part of his *visual* vocabulary. Just to make sure, I ask, 'What makes them fierce?'

'Because I draw them fierce.' Obligingly he shows me his two ways of drawing teeth, fierce and not fierce: one using diagonal lines, the other with lines going up, across and down.

I couldn't have hoped for a more perfect example of the power of a line. Merely by a change in direction, meanings can change.

This example showed me how early children become aware of the 'hows' of making an image, not just the 'what'.

SEE ALSO
Drawing **42**
Painting **53**

Discovering Shapes

Children are eager shape-makers. It's an exciting moment when they discover shapes emerge as they make a marker or brush go *around and around*.

Children love to repeat shape-making actions. For instance, long before he was three, Colin had a passion for making rectangles. Over months he explored 'rectangleness' with whatever materials were at hand. He drew rectangles, painted them, and made them with blocks and clay. He divided and subdivided them, or filled them in. With peers, he tackled rectangle-making on a grand scale using blocks. And once he and a friend constructed a 'giant swimming pool' – a rectangle made with coils of clay that spanned half a table.

Intriguing shape-making experiences occur whenever children draw, paint, cut paper, or work with dough and clay. This section describes a few.

POTENT SHAPES, MAGIC SHAPES

To young children the initial letter of their names is a potent shape, a magic shape. So is the numeral which stands for their age.

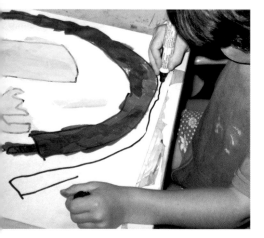 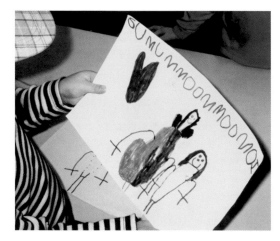

For young children drawing and writing are closely linked. Letter shapes often appear in their drawings.

VISUAL SURPRISE

Georgia (4 years 10 months) was so enraptured over her first paper cut-out that she wanted to rush home to show this technique to her brother. To help her remember how to teach it to him, we made up a chant: *Corner to corner, corner to corner. Fold and fold, and fold again. Then snip and snip!* (Fold the paper in half, then twice more. Cut out small shapes across the folds.)

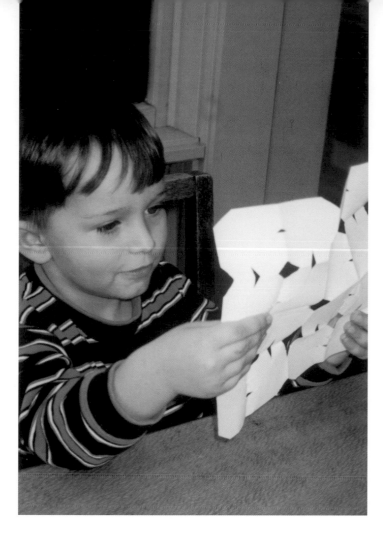

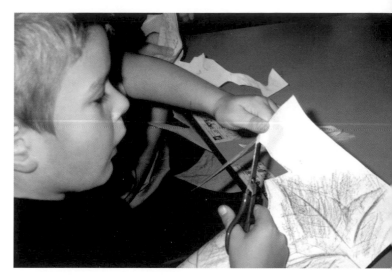

Visual surprise:
cuts in folded paper
produce magic when you
unfold the paper.

Hey, I made a star!
Cutting out his leaf rubbing,
a six-year-old is astonished
to discover a star-shaped
'see-through' shape.

HEY, I MADE A STAR!

As older children learn to cut out shapes using a continuous movement, they discover – to their surprise – that this results in both a cut-out shape and a remaining 'see-through' shape.

FAMILIAR ICONS

What do you do when children ask you how to draw an everyday shape like a heart?

As a heart is both an appealing symmetrical shape and an icon cherished by many, it is no wonder children want to draw hearts. But problems arise when they want their heart shapes to look like those made by adults. No matter how much you try to convince them that their own efforts are fine, by a certain age they become dissatisfied with their attempts. They know that there are specific conventions for drawing this shape and are determined to learn them. Mastering these conventions is for some a milestone to be passed – a bit like learning to skip.

Some children teach themselves by tracing or drawing around outlines. Others seek help. If asked, I talk the task through, breaking it down into steps. For example, when Lina (4 years 11 months) asked for help, we looked at a heart

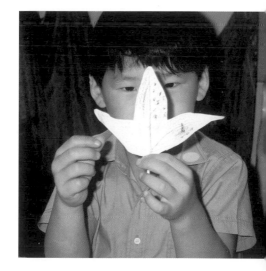

Seeing a leaf shape anew:
the ordinary becomes
extraordinary.

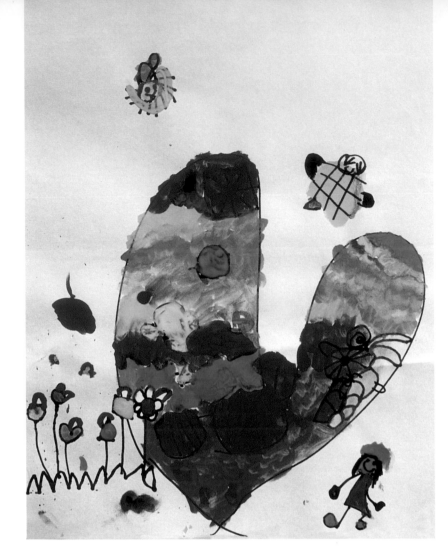

'The big heart is a colourful magic castle and I'm walking inside to see the queen of the bees. She's a magical bee so she has squares not stripes. There's lots of fairies too. The purple bit is the queen bee's butterfly and the pink bit is her caterpillar, and the caterpillar can even fly. The queen bee has a sun and it has a hat with a feather on it.' Painting by girl (4 years 11 months). Black felt-tip pen and thinned tempera paint applied with fine brush.

shape and imagined walking around it. *Start in the middle and go up, up and around. Then down, down on the diagonal to the point.* ('Diagonal' was a new word to her, but not a new concept.) *Then up, up again and around.* These words made the task seem manageable, and after a little practice she was soon drawing hearts that pleased her.

Some readers may be concerned that learning to draw hearts in this way involves following a formula. But I would argue that mastering a conventional heart shape is no different from learning to form letters. This is not the same as using a formula for drawing a human figure, an animal or object – which I would never do. Why? A formula robs children of the chance to think and see for themselves and create something new.

SEE ALSO
Discovering Patterns **33**
Discovering Light and Shadow **37**
Collage **76**
Printmaking **91**
Rubbings **95**

Discovering Forms

A wonderfully rich conversation among three- and four-year-olds around a clay table showed me how ideas can grow as children respond to forms – forms that emerge as they work with clay.

Amassing small pieces of clay into a large mound nearly 30 cm high, the children worked for over 45 minutes. During this time they shared and swapped ideas about mass, size, height, weight, texture and shape, as well as structure and balance – all qualities to do with forms. Here is an excerpt from their conversation about their collaborative effort, which became known as 'The Chocolate Hill'.

Steve: *(slicing a thick clay coil into segments with a paddle-pop stick)*
Hey, I'm making chocolates.

Leslie: I'm making chocolates too. Little ones.

Jed: Little ones and big ones. *(Adds pieces to a growing pile on a cardboard base provided by an adult watching their work.)*

Steve: I made a square one. We're making lots and lots of chocolates. It's getting bigger and bigger *(referring to the increasing mound)*. We'll have to 'tend [pretend] to eat it.

Leslie: It's getting higher and higher.

Steve: Let's make it up to the roof. That'll be heavy to carry.

Jed: Let's cover it *(referring to the cardboard base)*.

Steve: Hey, this piece is falling. Put them up here. Not there. No, no, up here.

Steve: *(to four-year-old Lisa passing by)* We're making chocolates.

Lisa: *(smiling)* A hundred chocolates!

Jed: They look like rocks you can climb all the way up.

Leslie: And we're making all this big thing.

Steve: A big hill. A big chocolate hill.

Jed: Bumpy rocks on the hill.

Steve: Chocolate rocks.

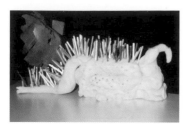

'Dinosaur' by a four-year-old.
The matchsticks depict 'spikes'
– an inventive solution to the
problem of depicting sharp
things with a soft material
like dough.

GENTLE FORMS

Damp sand, dough and clay invite children to make forms with soft edges.

Dough, like clay, invites children to make and remake forms. Dough, however, is softer and easier to handle than clay. It is ideal for toddlers to explore once they are past mouthing objects. (See page 130 for a recipe for dough.)

Clay, on the other hand, encourages children to explore form and structure on a larger scale and with more complexity. Favourite forms are balls, coils, bridges, columns and forms with holes.

Give children ample time to get the feel of dough and clay without using cookie cutters or rolling pins. Toddlers love to make forms they can squeeze, roll, bend, twist and flatten. If they're not distracted by tools, they quickly acquire skills – a language of hands.

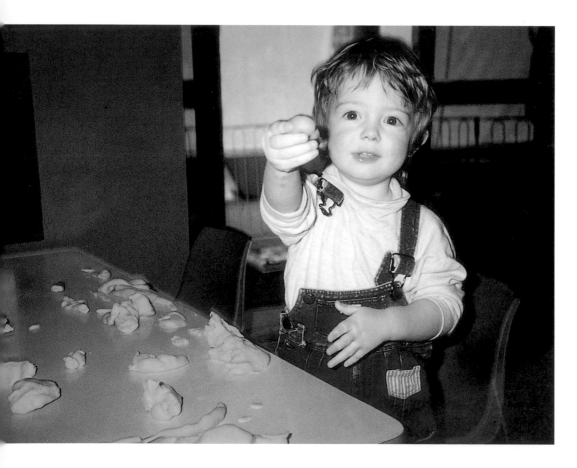

While curling a length of dough, a 22-month-old discovers a form reminding him of snails. 'Snail! snail!' he shouts, and promptly makes several more – his first representational forms with dough.

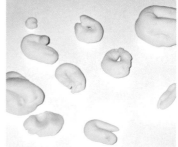

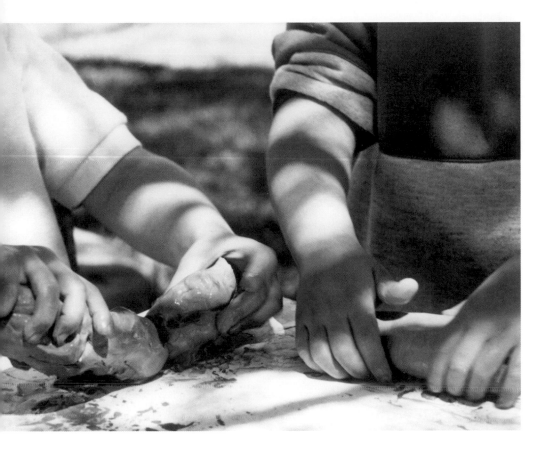

Clay forms.

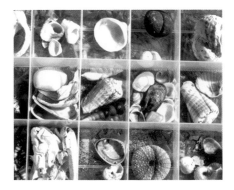

'It's a camera!' A three-year-old shows me how her 'camera' works. Her idea of making a camera arose from making a hole in the clay.

FOLDED AND CRUMPLED

In the hands of toddlers a sheet of paper changes into all sorts of forms. Watch what happens as toddlers fold, bundle, twist, crumple and scrunch paper (usually at lightning speed).

NATURAL FORMS

Natural forms tell stories about growth and weathering. A small gnarled tree stump, its roots twisting in all directions, and a sweet-smelling forked log are some of my treasures which children enjoy.

It's not necessary to make something with found materials. It is enough simply to display them. Let the intricacies of forms and textures spark children's curiosity. Of course, make sure that materials are non-toxic, cannot be swallowed and have no sharp pointed ends. Materials for very young children must be washable, wipeable or disposable.

HARD-EDGED FORMS

Hard-edged forms with smooth surfaces and corners, such as blocks and cardboard boxes, encourage children to build and construct.

Plain wooden blocks are wonderful materials. Their smooth, solid geometric forms have a beauty that appeals to both eye and hand. Boxes are evocative forms. Whether they might be for hiding treasures or creeping into, boxes appeal to the imagination. A box can become anything!

SQUARE AND ROUND, CURLY AND TWISTY

The poem, *Animals' Houses*, draws attention to form and shape in a most delightful way.

ANIMALS' HOUSES

Of animals' houses
  Two sorts are found -
Those which are square ones
  And those which are round.

Square is a hen-house,
  A kennel, a sty:
Cows have square houses
  And so have I.

A snail's shell is curly,
  A bird's nest round;
Rabbits have twisty burrows
  Underground.

But the fish in the bowl
  And the fish at sea -
Their houses are round
  As a house can be.

JAMES REEVES

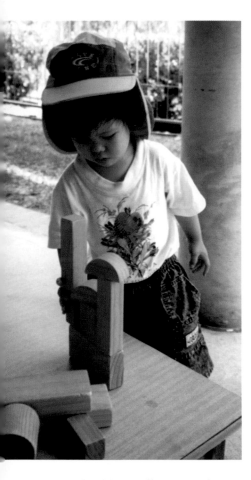

Wooden blocks offer wonderful opportunities for playing with geometric forms.

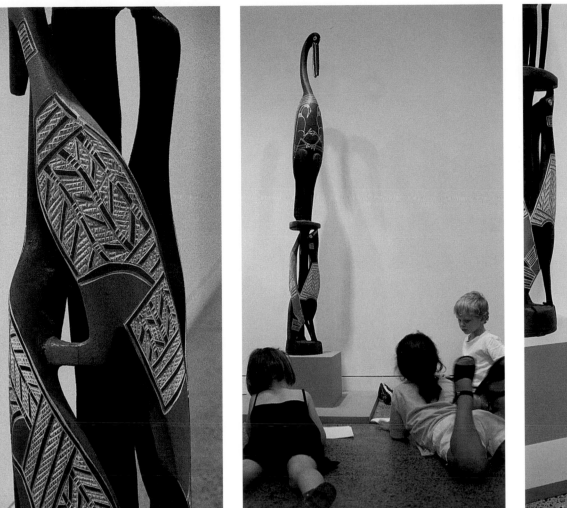
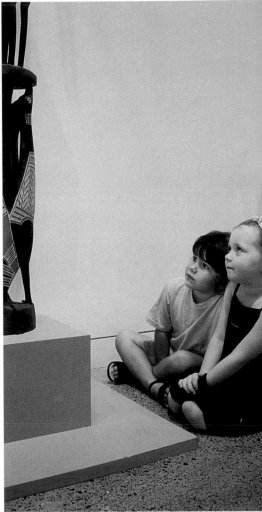

Dhukal Wirrpanda and
Galuma Maymuru (Australian)
Dhangultji at Dhuruputjpi, 1996
Natural pigments on wood

Courtesy of the artists and Art Gallery
of New South Wales, Sydney

CARVED FORMS

Carved forms have a special beauty. This sculpture of Dhangultji the Brolga with her chicks was made by the celebrated husband-wife team, Dhukal Wirrpanda and Galuma Maymuru, who live and work in Dhuruputjpi, about 200 kilometres from Yirrkala in Arnhem Land. During creation times the brolgas were ancestral beings who used to walk between the waterholes in the flood plains of this area. Later they transformed themselves into brolgas which still live there. The sacred weed associated with this part of the country, called Darranggi, has been incised on Dhangultji's tail and on her chicks.

SEE ALSO
Discovering Shapes **18**
Discovering Textures **31**
Discovering Patterns **33**
Claywork **66**
Building and Construction **84**

Discovering Colours

'The most beautiful object ... was a crystal candlestick, which was bracketed to the wall in the drawing room and from which crystal pendants hung. I would sit beneath it and stare, entranced, while lamplight pierced the pendants, shedding prismatic colour on wall and floor. For the want of a better term I must describe it as my first awareness of the aesthetic beauty of colour.' — *Lloyd Rees*

Lloyd Rees (1895 - 1988), a great Australian artist, remembers a childhood experience in *Peaks and Valleys*, Collins, Sydney, 1985, p.10.

THE WONDER OF MIXING AND MAKING

To play with colour is to play with magic.

Look! It's getting paler and paler!
Simon (2 years 10 months) adding lemon yellow to dark green paint.

Hey, I made a purplish black!
Lee (3 years 5 months) mixing black and crimson.

It's a rainbow colour! I put yellow on it and then it went on the red and I made the rainbow colour. Lachlan (4 years).

When you paint a colour on top of a colour, you make other colours.
Laura (4 years 1 month).

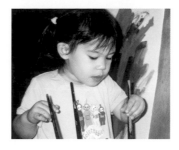

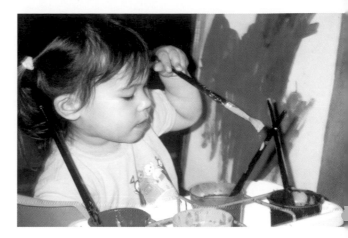

To mix and make colours is engrossing and emotionally satisfying.

COLOUR LANGUAGE

I was fascinated when Jessica (2 years 10 months) showed a liking for a new mustard-yellow paint at the easel. When I told her its name, yellow ochre, she immediately chanted 'Ochre-ochre-ochre!' She then insisted that she 'write' her name on her ochre painting with an ochre colour and trotted off in search of a felt-tipped pen. At the drawing table where the pens were kept (out of view of the easel) she paused to stare at two fairly similar yellow pens. Then, despite having no example of ochre to refer to, she seized the shade closest to ochre and ran back to write her name.

From an early age children are able to discriminate between colours, and between shades of one colour. They show colour preferences and a remarkable ability for colour memory – that is, they remember actual colours, if not always their names.

The more words children learn to use for describing colours, the more they can tell you what they notice and think about colours. For instance, when four-year-old Maria looked at clouds in a photograph, she gave a delightful and accurate description: 'They're a pinkish, purplish blue'.

FROM GENTLE PASTELS TO VIVID JEWEL COLOURS

Playing with fabrics offers children opportunities to perceive colour nuances – from gentle pastels to vivid jewel colours.

I watched this infant make a beeline for these scarves. Abandoned on the floor by toddlers who had draped themselves with them, the scarves drew him like a magnet. Utterly enchanted, he revelled in the colourful soft silkiness for many minutes.

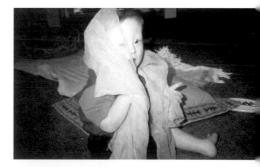

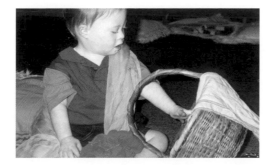

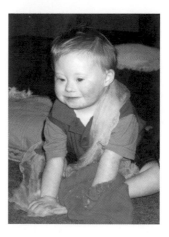

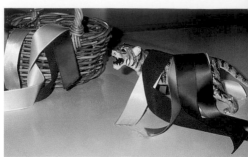

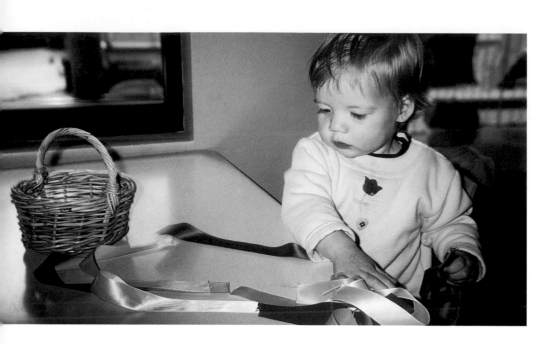

A selection of ribbons in pairs of colours kept young toddlers (22 - 24 months) entranced for almost half an hour. In their hands the ribbons became a 'leaf falling', 'noodles', a 'blanket' for a toy tiger and 'rain' as they danced with them, chanting 'Raining! Raining!'

COLOURS IN THE LANDSCAPE

A feast of subtle colours can be found outdoors.

Fallen frangipani blooms.

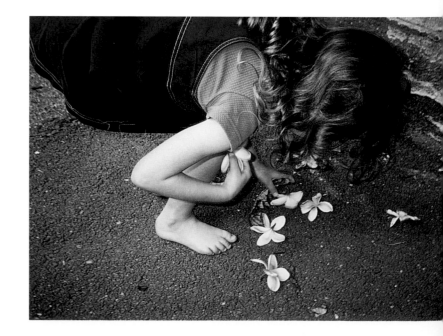

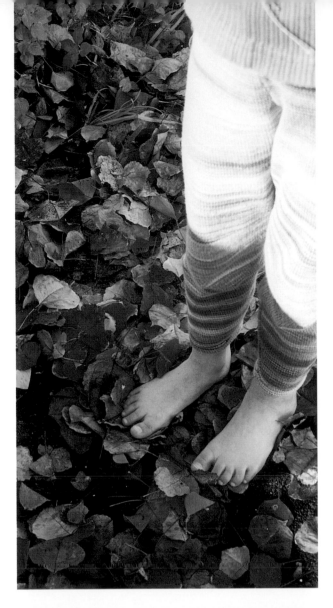

Children intuitively respond to the
fragile beauty of seasonal colours.

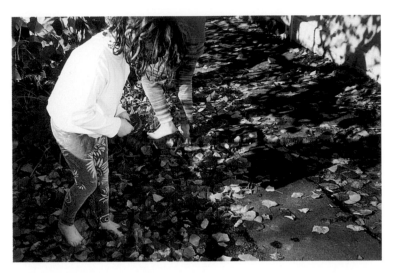

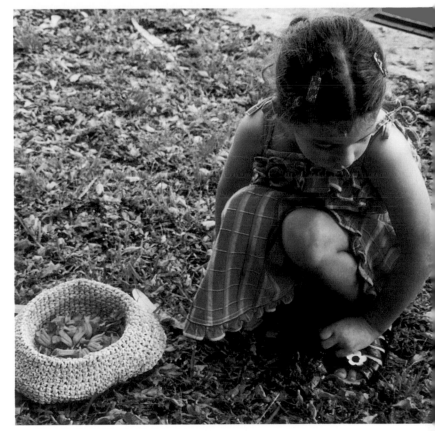

A carpet of purpleness under
a jacaranda tree.

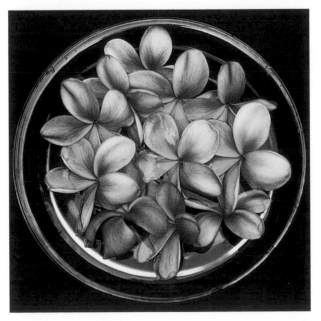

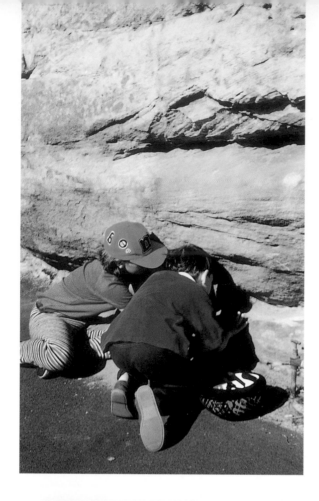

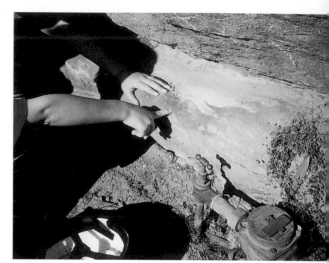

Look at the different colours in rocks! Where do they come from? An outcrop of Sydney sandstone on a suburban street yields a sprinkling of sand in glorious rusts, reddish-golds, palest pinks, creams and ochres.

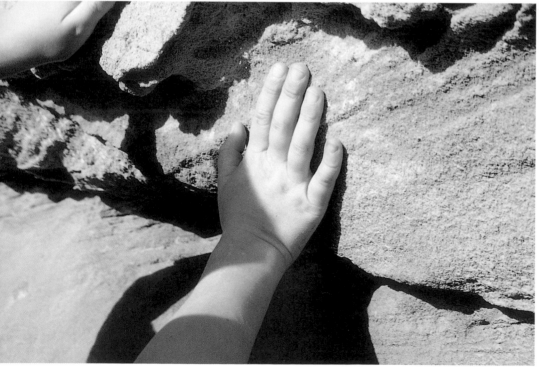

Discovering Textures

Among a baby's earliest experiences is the feel of things against skin. Through the sense of touch, children learn about their world. Long before they learn words like 'rough', 'smooth', 'hard' or 'soft', they have reached out to touch countless textured surfaces. They have learned to recognise qualities and distinguish between them.

POUNDING AND PRESSING, PINCHING AND INCISING

Pounding and pressing, caressing and smoothing, pinching and incising – children soon discover such actions transform a clay surface. They also become aware of accidental textures. 'Hey! Look at this! Look what I made!' Peeling away a lump of clay from a canvas tablecloth, Claire finds an imprint on the underside. Pressed into the clay is a perfect impression of the woven cloth!

DABBING AND STROKING, GLIDING AND TWIRLING

As they paint, children discover that different actions produce different marks and textures. This can inspire them to investigate further.

Finding out what a brush can do is fascinating. Try to picture it from a child's point of view: in the hand is a long, hard unbending stick that ends in a tuft of soft, flexible bristles or hairs that can make a splat, or glide, stroke and sweep, or maybe even twirl into delicate traceries.

For a finger-painter, swirling fingers lusciously through colour is an even greater tactile experience. Incidentally, there's no need to add substances like sand or sawdust to produce texture. Additives usually make paint a less sensuous medium because it becomes difficult for children to use. My advice is to offer paint that is smooth and flowing.

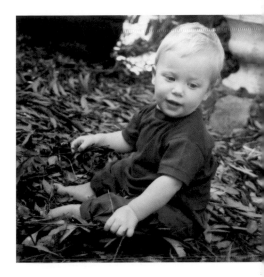

Through the sense of touch children learn about the world: tactile sensations often remain longer in the memory than visual ones.

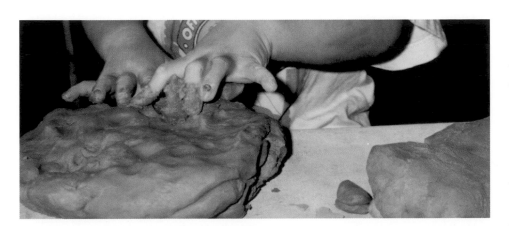

Pounding clay with her finger tips, a three-year-old sees a texture appear. This makes her think of rain and she begins to bounce up and down. 'Raindrops! Raindrops! I'm making raindrops!' she chants, rhythmically peppering the clay with tiny indentations. It's a lovely example of how chance textures can spark an idea.

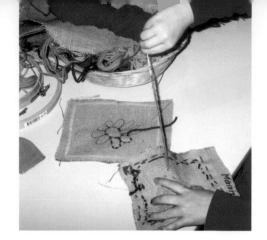

Stitching on hessian (burlap) with thick tapestry needles and wool is a challenging experience as well as a richly tactile one.

SILKY AND SATINY, VELVETY AND WOOLLY

Gorgeous dress-up clothes and filmy chiffon scarves, laces and ribbons, wools and yarns offer a feast of textures that beckon to be stroked.

FEATHERY AND FURRY, KNOBBLY AND STONY

Many natural materials have appealing or intriguing textures. When collecting objects for very young children, make sure that items are safe, not able to be swallowed, and washable, wipeable or replaceable.

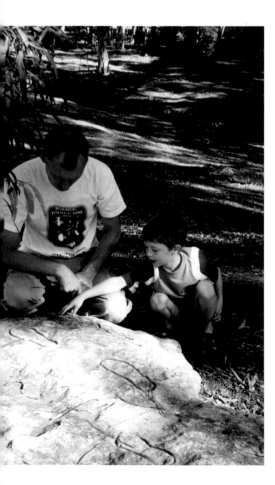

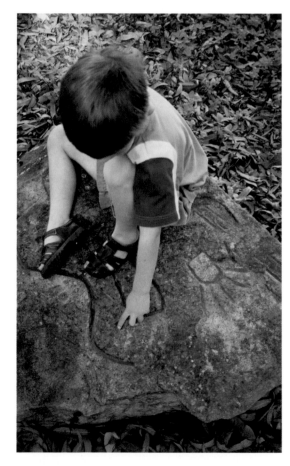

This rock is one of nine in *Water is Life* in the Sculpture Park at Macquarie University – the work of Darug artists Edna Mariong Watson and Patricia Karbo Jarvis. Engraved with symbols representing the tracks of animals and Darug women, the rocks are arranged in a serpentine fashion winding down towards a creek.

Edna Mariong Watson and **Patricia Karbo Jarvis** (Australian)
Water is Life, 1999 (section)

Courtesy of the artists and Macquarie University, Sydney

SEE ALSO
Painting **53**
Claywork **66**
Collage **76**
Rubbings **95**

Discovering Patterns

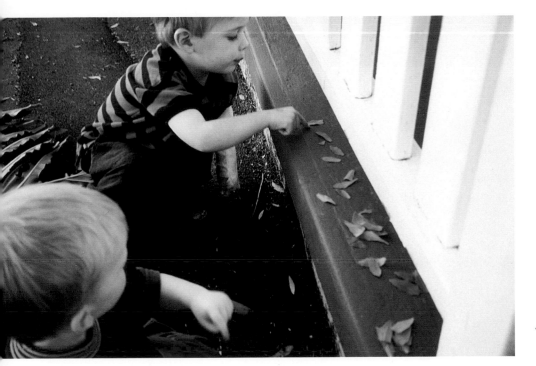

An arrangement of leaves:
a caterpillar's 'dinner'

Children love arranging and ordering things. For instance, a three-year-old and a two-year-old, out on a walk with their mother, stopped to watch a caterpillar. Soon the children were utterly absorbed in arranging leaves for its 'dinner'. Commented their mother: 'It was interesting watching what they did with the leaves – each had his own way of arranging them. Andy made groupings, and Stan laid them out evenly, one by one. They must've spent about twenty minutes on this!'

HOORAY!

Our eyes are drawn to patterns around us. A scene in a day care centre once showed me this vividly. It occurred at a table abandoned by toddlers, who had left it strewn with lumps of playdough. I reworked the dough into small balls, but instead of making a pile in the centre of the table, I arranged eight balls in a row. I then stood back, leaving the arrangement to provoke ideas (or be ignored).

The first passer-by was 22-month-old Adam, who had been among the earlier players. As soon as he saw the row of balls, he stopped in his tracks, smiled at them and sat down. Delicately, almost gingerly, he lifted the first ball.

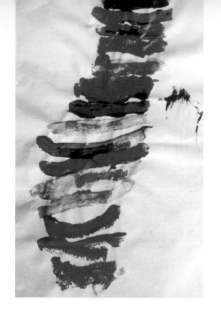

Stroke follows stroke: you can almost feel the pulse, the rhythm. Making and looking at patterns engages mind and eye. For many, pattern-making is deeply satisfying. Patterns may also have meanings; on completion many children think of titles for them.

Without disturbing the others, he placed it in front of him and remoulded it into a sort of pancake. He then took the next ball, placed it precisely next to the first and remoulded it too. Slowly he repeated this sequence six more times. Then utterly enchanted, he gazed at his line of identical shapes, raised his arms in the air and shouted 'Hooray!'

I've often thought about that *Hooray* – and what sparked it. It showed me how important it is for children to repeat actions rhythmically and see patterns emerge.

PATTERN PAINTING

In children's arrangements of lines and dots you see a delight in repeating them in rows. This is often the beginning of pattern painting.

Sometimes adults find it difficult to know what to say to a young pattern-maker because a pattern does not depict something recognisable or tell a story. However, try saying: *You've painted this very carefully – how did you start?*

Children's answers often reveal that they seem to be playing what I call 'visual games'. I use the word 'game' because pattern-making, like a game, is governed by rules. Of course the child invents the rules. And this is why pattern-making is so fascinating.

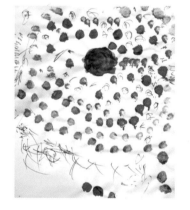

'Footprints when me and Dad went walking in the mud'.

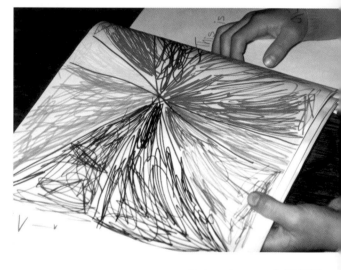

Radial patterns are common.

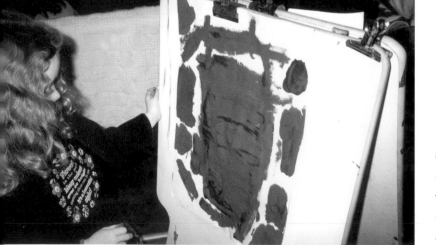

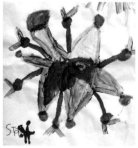

Children enjoy creating symmetrical arrangements: they often place similar shapes on either side of a central axis.

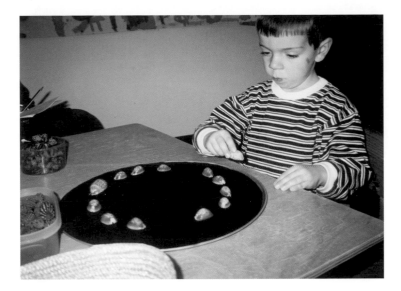

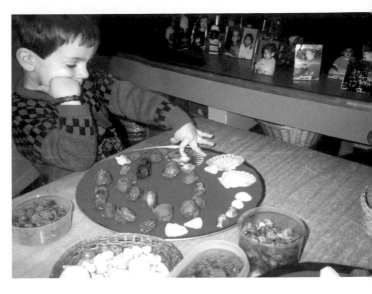

Arranging natural objects on a bed of felt invites sensuous handling and contemplation. Although the arrangements are temporary, photographs create a lasting record.

ARE THEY REAL?

When four-year-old Rachel first sat down to make patterns with shells, she studied them carefully. 'Are they real?' she asked. On being reassured that they were, she checked again: 'They real shells, not 'tend [pretend] shells?'

I'm not sure what prompted Rachel's question, but I think the 'realness' of objects like shells and seedpods (as opposed to manufactured items) makes them fascinating for children. Pattern-making with these objects seems to invite contemplation, a sort of 'slowed-down' looking. Children seem to enter into a dialogue with nature.

With no glue used, the objects in the photographs simply nestle on felt. Freed from the distraction of gluing, children are able to focus on choosing, arranging and rearranging. Importantly, they have time to notice patterns on the objects.

Pattern-making with found objects is best suited for children close to four or older. You need large quantities of objects in three or four basic shapes: for example, long skinny shapes, large round shapes, and small conical shapes. Children need a sufficient number of the *same* few contrasting shapes to make interesting arrangements. Choose from materials such as shells, seedpods, walnut shells, short twigs, feathers or pine needles. Make sure that items are non-toxic and cannot be swallowed.

Begin by sorting materials with children, letting them decide on categories for sorting. For instance, spiral shapes might go in one container, fan shapes in another.

For bases, you can line trays or shallow boxes with pieces of felt. Alternatively, fill deep trays with damp sand.

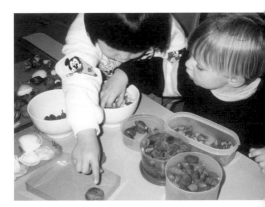

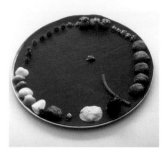

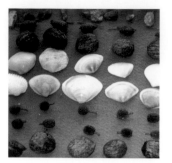

Arrangements by four-year-olds of shells, casuarina pods and walnut shells. The children's sensitivity to the beauty of these objects shows in the way they have arranged them. A lovely example of 'letting nature speak'.

TILES, TAPA CLOTH AND EASTER EGGS

Pattern-making has been a part of most cultures since ancient times and children are interested in examples from all round the world.

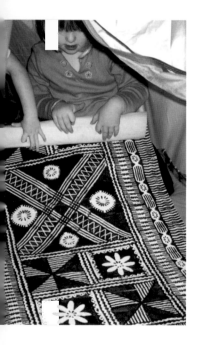

Patterns on tapa cloth from Fiji. Tapa cloth, a traditional art form in the Pacific Islands, is used for clothing, decorating houses and gift-giving. The material is the underbark of the paper mulberry tree, pounded into paper-thin sheets. Colours in the designs come from pigments derived from various trees.

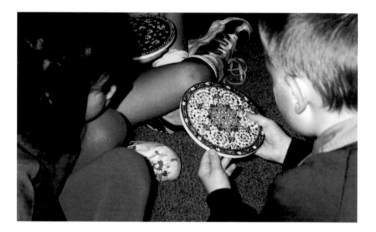

Tiles from Iran. Geometrical patterns have been central to Islamic art for centuries. From awe-inspiring architecture to intricate carpets, Islamic art has reached extraordinary heights in pattern-making.

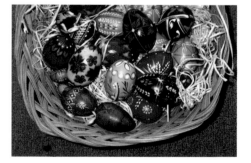

A classroom display of hand-carved wooden Easter eggs from Poland.

SEE ALSO
Painting **53**
Printmaking **91**
Rubbings **95**

Discovering Light and Shadow

FLETCHER AVENUE

In my
grandmother's house
sun comes through leaded panes
on the front stair landing, creeping
softly

over
the red carpet,
flashing yellow circles
and white dots, with ribbons of blue
dancing

on the
banisters and
balconies, coming to
rest on warm wood walls in the dark
hallways.

MYRA COHN LIVINGSTON

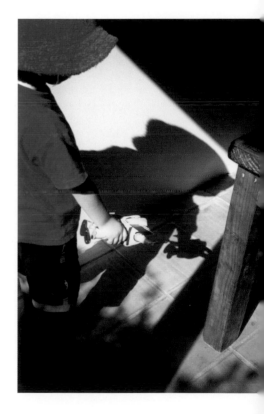

'Come look at the sky! Come look, come look!' cried three-year-old Tim, tugging at my sleeve. It had been a dark, dank afternoon at the day care centre until a sudden change in the light outside drew Tim onto the verandah. Following his lead, a few three-year-olds and I rushed outside. Brilliant grey-violet light pierced a low blanket of black cloud, bathing everything with an eerie luminosity. Our faces shone greenly as we gazed around in wonder. In the distance thunder rumbled. And then fat raindrops began to plop on our upturned faces. We ran back inside, and at the drawing table, using black markers, the children drew raindrops, whole sheets of falling raindrops.

The Swedish film director Ingmar Bergman once said to an interviewer: 'All of us collect fortunes when we are children – a fortune of colours, of lights and darkness, of movements, of tensions. Some of us have the fantastic chance to go back to this fortune when grown up.'

Playing with his toy spaceman, a three-year-old stops to investigate its shadow.

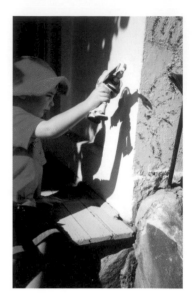

When you see shadows cast, you often see things you didn't notice before.

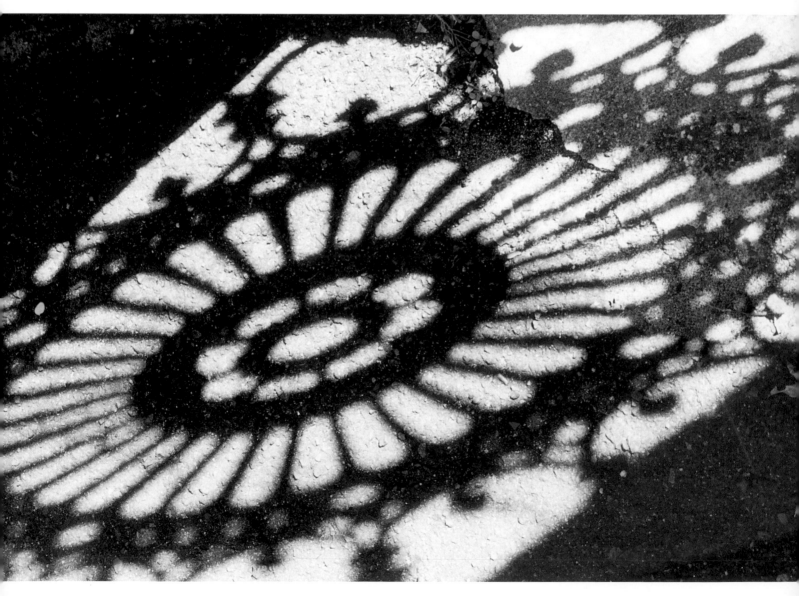

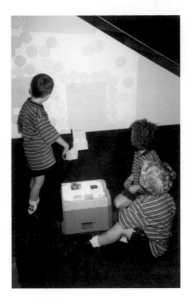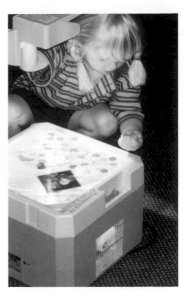

MAKING SHADOWS

Jamie was a crawling infant whose teacher noticed that he regularly manoeuvred himself into a certain spot on the nursery floor. Here he would make shadows by waving his hands in a patch of lamplight. Intrigued, I sat in Jamie's exact spot. It was then that I found he had selected the best spot: from this position he could see shadows at their most intense.

CORROBOREE

Hot day dies, cook time comes,
Now between the sunset and the sleeptime
Time of play about.
The hunters paint black bodies by firelight with
    designs of meaning,
To dance corroboree.
Now didgeridoo compels with haunting drone
    eager feet to stamp,
Click-sticks click in rhythm to swaying bodies
Dancing corroboree.
Like Spirit things in from the great surrounding
    dark
Ghost gums dimly seen stand at the edge of
    light
Watching corroboree.
Eerie the scene in leaping firelight,
Eerie the sounds in that wild setting
As naked dancers weave stories of the tribe
Into corroboree.

OODGEROO OF THE TRIBE NOONUCCAL

'We're making a story with shadows,' the children tell me as they arrange transparent, translucent and solid coloured objects on an overhead projector.

Reflected light is another wonder that gives great pleasure. Many adults may remember a time when they collected shiny things – collecting dewdrops to make a tiny silvery puddle in a nasturtium leaf cup was one of my favourite pastimes.

SILVER

Slowly, silently, now the moon
Walks the night in her silver shoon;
This way, and that, she peers, and sees
Silver fruit upon silver trees;
One by one the casements catch
Her beams beneath the silvery thatch;
Couched in his kennel, like a log,
With paws of silver sleeps the dog;
From their shadowy cote the white breasts peep
Of doves in a silver-feathered sleep;
A harvest mouse goes scampering by,
With silver claws, and silver eye;
And moveless fish in the water gleam,
By silver reeds in a silver stream.

WALTER DE LA MARE

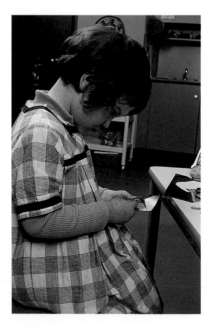

Light reflected from a gold fragment creates a moment of wonder. An 'ordinary' collage experience becomes extraordinary.

Kinds of Image-making

Images are either flat (like drawings and most paintings), three-dimensional (like sculptures) or a combination of flat and three-dimensional parts (like some kinds of collage or contemporary painting). This chapter gives information on the kinds of image-making of greatest use to young children for exploring, representing and communicating their thoughts.

Rather than thinking of children's image-making as 'art', it may be more helpful to see it in a different light. Just as adults use notes and diagrams to assist understanding, so children use images to make sense of things and play with ideas.

But, you might ask, what about the drawings children make of fantastical things, the impossible, the hilariously nonsensical? How do these imaginary worlds help them make sense of the real world? The best answer I've found comes from the Russian poet and writer, Kornei Chukovsky*. In his book *From Two to Five*, he looks at how young children think and, in particular, discusses their delight in nonsense verse or 'topsy turvies' as he calls them. He observes that children relish jokes about an 'upside-down world' precisely because they know the real order of things. Fantasies and topsy-turvies of all kinds actually help children to play with ideas about the real world.

* Kornei Chukovsky, *From Two to Five*, University of California Press, Berkeley, 1971.

Drawing

Of all the visual arts, drawing is the quickest and most direct way of making ideas visible. It is an incredibly powerful tool – a language – that enables children to explain things to themselves and to others. Drawing often intertwines with painting, but it's also very different. It lets children make marks with an immediacy, directness and precision that can't be matched with paint.

My son Paul was five when he first saw mountains, and he was so amazed that he made drawing after drawing of them. For him, having grown up on a vast plain, these towering mountains were more than spectacular. They completely changed his understanding of the world. No wonder he had to draw – it was a way of coming to terms with 'mountainness'. His excitement made him draw. He drew in order to learn and understand.

APPRECIATING WHAT CHILDREN DO

The impulse to make marks begins early. With fingers and whatever materials are at hand – food, mud, a steamed-up window, crayons or markers – infants and young toddlers discover a relationship between their actions and the marks that appear.

At first glance a toddler's actions may seem random. But take a closer look. In the sequence below, the child has just exchanged a red pen for a black one. She starts to investigate what it can do and immediately notices something. Pointing to a mark, she says something inaudible. What has she noticed? Unfortunately I don't know. Transferring the pen to her right hand, she draws on top of her red marks, pauses to look at the result and then turns to another empty space. Clearly her actions are not merely random. As an investigator she is remarkably thorough, and *learning to look intently* is a vital part of her experience.

Mark-making at 20 months of age: *making something visible that wasn't there before.* This is not 'just scribbling'. It's an engrossing experience that demands this toddler's total attention and concentration. It's also a wonderfully self-affirming experience: *look what I've done!* And it's about learning how to hold a pen and how to make marks on paper and not on the table.

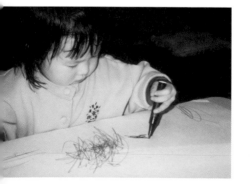
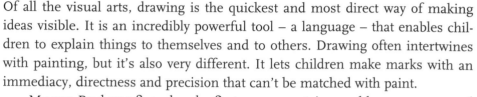
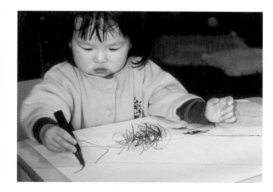

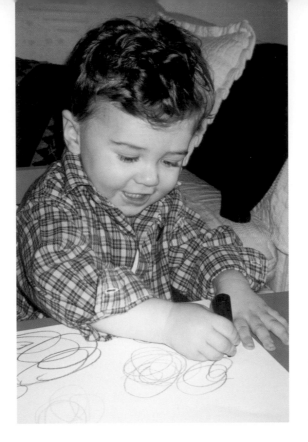

Absorbed in using his new skill in making circular shapes, a 22-month-old makes one after another.

At some point children make a remarkable discovery: mere marks on a piece of paper can *stand for* things not actually present. For instance, a mark or shape may remind them of something. They may name a mark or shape *ball* or *snail* – even though to our eyes it's 'only a scribble'.

Although the early named drawings don't seem to resemble anything, the achievement is significant. Why? By labelling marks and shapes, children show they understand that marks can communicate. They are at the threshold of learning to make images, letters and numbers.

We shouldn't judge children's drawings according to adult ideas about realistic pictures. Children don't aim to achieve realism in the sense that we understand it. And the actual marks on paper are often only *part* of the activity. If you overlook the accompanying gestures, sounds and words, you may get only half the meaning. Children know far more than they can convey in a drawing.

Marks might briefly stand for a person, an animal or an object, and then become something else. They might stand for phenomena, such as the sound of thunder growing louder and louder, or the jumping movements of a creature. A drawing might represent the noise, speed and movement of an aeroplane as well as its shape, or it might simply represent its flight path. A child may blithely announce that she is drawing the wind – an idea not as fanciful as it may seem if we think of meteorologists' weather maps.

After a lot of experimentation children discover how to make a single closed shape. This takes concentration and skill, and they practise this shape over and over again.

Children gradually add to their repertoire of shapes, and some of these begin to resemble humans, animals or objects. Then we may recognise the intention in a drawing.

How do children tackle the daunting task of depicting a three-dimensional world in just a few lines? The following incident in a preschool offered me a glimpse into this process.

Andrew's bird Andrew was just three when he urgently announced, 'I want to draw a bird'. His manner implied: *and I want you to help me.*

I must explain that Andrew had recently discovered he could draw a person. (I use the word 'person' because children's early figures are typically sexless, or interchangeably male/female as the drawing progresses or is 'told' to a viewer.) By adding to a basic circular shape two dots for eyes, a line for a mouth, and two lines for legs, Andrew found he could make something recognisable to others. Of course he *knew* a good deal more about bodies than his drawings conveyed; however, this was what he was able to draw. But now he had a new goal. Having watched four-year-olds draw birds, cut them out and place them in an empty bird-cage, he wanted to draw a bird too. Unfortunately the bird drawers (who might have helped him) were elsewhere. Andrew was alone at the table. Our dialogue continued something like this.

'Good idea,' I said, and moved the pens closer to him. Andrew scowled. 'I don't know how!' I responded with encouraging words. He scowled even more. I tried to engage him in a discussion about birds and found a picture of a bird. To no avail. He was furious. It seemed that I was avoiding the central issue: *how do you draw a bird?* I knew that I was failing. Andrew was kicking the table.

In desperation, I asked: 'Would you like me to *tell* you how to draw a bird?' Relief flooded across his face. Unsure that this approach was appropriate (since I'd never tried it before), I hesitated. Then I took the plunge. 'I think you need to start with a shape. Can you make a shape?'

Instantly Andrew drew a circular shape and looked up at me cheerfully, pen poised. 'If it's going to fly, what will it need?' I asked. 'Wings,' he said happily, and drew a horizontal line on each side of the shape. Then, smiling to himself, he added a third line at the top of the shape and said, 'I'm making his beak.' For him, the bird was complete.

From then on, he was content to make drawing after drawing of birds. Within days and weeks his birds acquired eyes, legs and feet, as well as babies in nests and worms in their beaks.

This little episode taught me a lot. By using the same circular shape and the same two lines that he used for making people, but this time in a different configuration, Andrew showed me how children use a basic 'vocabulary' to suit different purposes.

He also showed me that when children say they don't know how to draw something, they probably mean: *I don't know how to start.* What they require is someone – perhaps a slightly more experienced child – to help them sort out a strategy. They certainly don't need an adult to draw for them. When children tell us they want to draw a bird, for example, we can't assume that we know what they have in mind. Had I drawn a bird for Andrew, he would have been no nearer to knowing how to draw one himself.

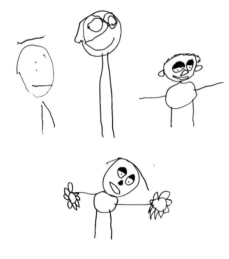

At first children use a single shape to stand for both head and body. What looks to us like a 'head' we should think of as a 'head/torso'. Children frequently omit arms in these early drawings, possibly because they work from the top downwards and forget to go back up to do the arms. In time, however, they discover ways of including a separate torso with arms and other features.

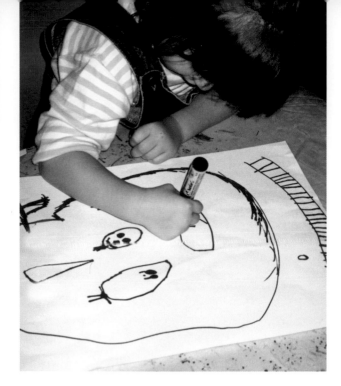

This drawing shows some typical early human figures.

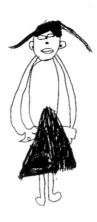

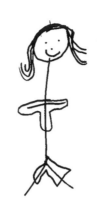

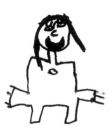

These drawings by four- to six-year-olds show some of the solutions children arrive at when depicting figures from memory.

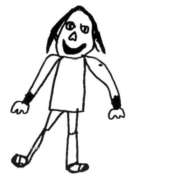

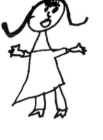

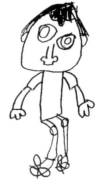

Relationships When children begin to include recognisable landscape features, such as trees and houses, they often appear to float in space. However, in time children begin to relate figures, animals and objects to each other, to a ground line at the bottom of the sheet, and to a sky line at the top.

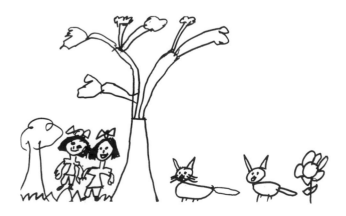

Here the figures and objects relate to each other as well as to a ground line.

45

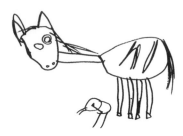

Profiles Gradually children work out how to draw heads in profile. This means they have to abandon their usual way of drawing, which is not an easy thing to do. To draw a head in profile means drawing a head with only one eye, and at first this feels 'wrong'.

When five-year-old Brandon drew his first profile (a dinosaur's head), he seemed to need approval from his friend Nick, whom he considered an expert drawer. 'I'm only drawing one eye,' he said. 'Yes,' said Nick, 'that's because the other one's at the back of his head.'

Drawing a head in profile means drawing it with only one eye. This feels 'wrong' at first.

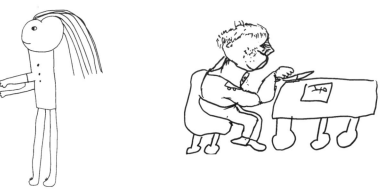

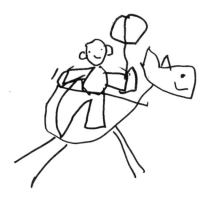

Stories unfolding in space and time Enthralled by videos of *Star Wars*, a trio spend days drawing as they retell events from the story and exchange information about space travel. Although experienced picture-makers, on this occasion they choose to make different kinds of images. Instead of drawing recognisable pictures with a right way up, they draw flight paths and events occurring at high speed, including trajectories of hurtling objects - all accompanied with explosive vocal sound effects.

They even make signs to indicate future happenings. As one boy explains to me, pointing to a circular mark: 'This one hasn't exploded yet – these others have happened – but this one isn't exploded yet.'

Star Wars, felt-tip pen, by four- to five-year-olds.

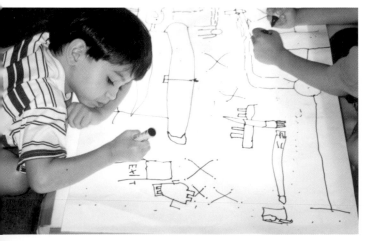

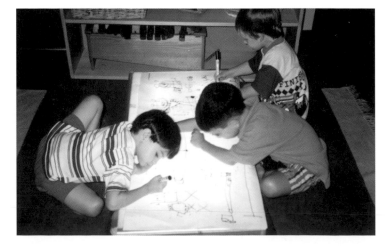

- Often you don't have to say anything while children draw. Merely being close at hand, watching and listening with genuine interest, does wonders. Sitting beside children makes the experience special.

- If children want a verbal reaction, try affirming what they have done. For example, *I see you've made a lot of lines.* Often the best comment is simply: *I see you're working very carefully!* At other times it may be helpful to ask: *I wonder what's happening here - would you like to tell me?*

- Should you show young children how to hold a marker correctly? If a child achieves clear marks despite an 'incorrect' grip, it would be a mistake to correct him or her at that moment. Many children lose interest when someone interrupts their train of thought. But offer help if a child's grip results in pale marks.

- Keep in mind that children develop drawing skills at their own pace. Some have opportunities to begin before the age of two, others not till much later. Some children draw every day, others rarely. Some are reluctant because they lack confidence. Others prefer to explore ideas in a different medium, such as clay.

I don't know what to draw! Sometimes children's minds are so abuzz with ideas that they can't focus on any one topic. Give them new materials to experiment with such as white chalk on black paper. Their first playful marks may trigger ideas.

I've finished! You often hear this from five- and six-year-olds on completing a drawing within seconds. When children are unfamiliar with the idea that they can take time over a drawing, they often try to impress you with their speed (they may also be hiding feelings of insecurity). Your response might be: *You're a fast worker! Now take another look – I wonder if your next drawing can show other things you've noticed. Take your time – you can do lots of drawings.*

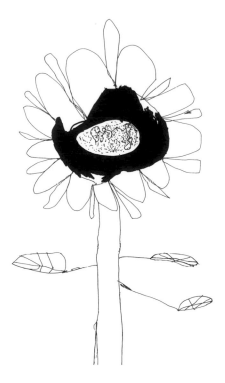

I don't know how to draw it! Take this complaint seriously. It often means that a child doesn't know how to start. Sometimes talking through the steps of drawing is helpful. For example, when five-year-old Sam was in a rage about his efforts to draw a dinosaur, he calmed down when we looked at pictures of dinosaurs and toy dinosaurs and talked calmly about what he could see and how he might start.

He/she tears up half-finished drawings, one after the other, in frustration. Older children sometimes believe that they have to 'get it right' the first time, or they become frustrated because their drawings don't look 'real'. Explain that drawers often don't get it right the first time. Just as some people practise catching balls hundreds of times, so drawers learn to draw by making hundreds of drawings. Try suggesting they do a number of 'drafts' by putting tracing paper over the first drawing. To those struggling to draw something from memory, say, a bicycle, suggest they look at a real one.

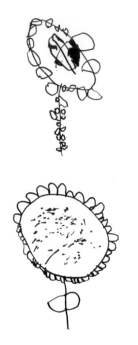

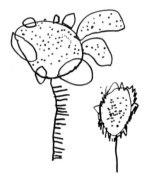

'Sunflowers', felt-tip pen, by three- and four-year-olds. The presence of giant sunflowers inspires children to make several drawings each.

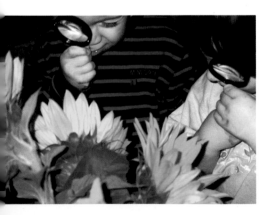

Drawing from observation Drawing from observation means drawing something while looking at it. Until fairly recently this was frowned on by early childhood educators, who thought it would discourage creativity and stifle the imagination. They also thought it was too difficult for young children to do. Happily these notions are changing.

Many now agree that this kind of drawing delights experienced drawers. It invites children to look closely at things and encourages them to make more detailed drawings than they do when drawing from memory. It can also lead to joyful discoveries. For instance, a four-year-old, peering intently at a sunflower before starting to draw, exclaimed, 'The petals are bursting out of the flower!'

Here are some points to keep in mind.

- Don't expect children to make more 'realistic' drawings. While they are likely to include more details than they usually do, they will still use their normal style of drawing.

- Find something that interests children. It should have a simple shape similar to ones they already know how to draw. For example, the circular head of a sunflower resembles shapes children often draw. A rose, on the other hand, has a complex shape and so is more difficult to draw.

- Invite children to talk about the object. Share with them your own pleasure in its shapes and patterns and encourage them to try drawing it. Be aware that simply talking about an object and seeing and touching it can be enough for some children.

- Let children tackle observational drawing in their own ways. If it's new to them, they may disregard the object and draw something else from memory.

- Remind children from time to time to look at the object in front of them.

- Even for a skilled drawer, drawing from observation is never a matter of only 'copying what you see'. It always involves interaction between seeing and reasoning, feeling and memory. Each person 'sees' differently, each chooses different parts to draw.

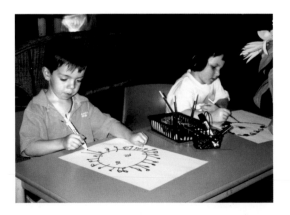

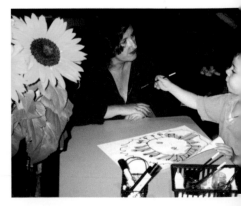

In order to draw the sunflower's long stem, this child taped a second piece of paper to his first.

A wooden manikin (obtainable from artists' shops) encourages a group of four- and five-year-olds to depict movement in figures. This is not easy. In order to draw limbs bent at the joints, children have to abandon using their usual straight lines – a challenging thing to do.

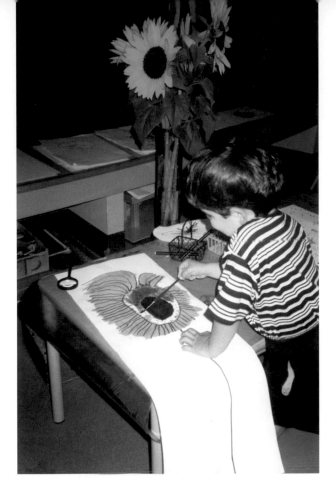

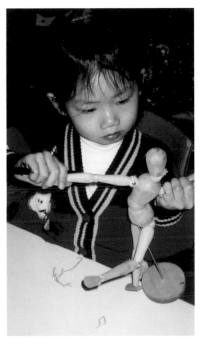

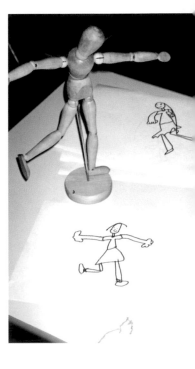

Pictures of magnified details of a sunflower add interest to the experience.

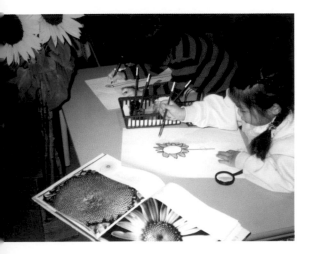

The unexpected find of an insect (a praying mantis) inspires serious study by four- and five-year-olds.

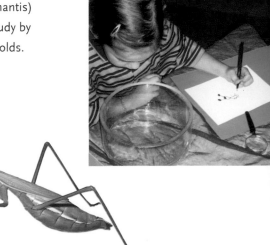

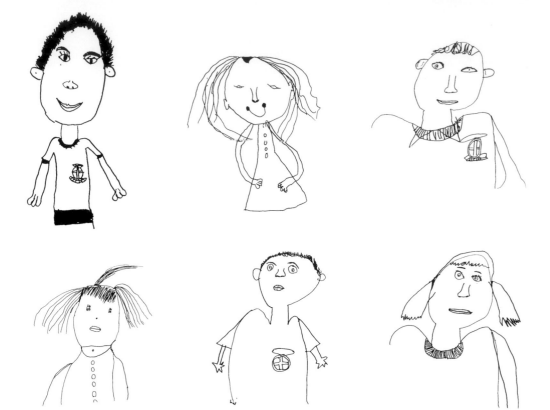

Drawing from observation: portraits of friends by five- and six-year-olds, felt-tip pen.

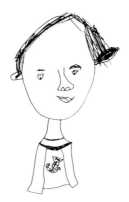

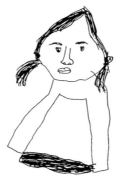

Cut-out drawings A good way to spark new ideas is to encourage children to cut out their drawings, or photocopies of them. You may need to offer help with cutting. Cutting out creates visual surprise and excites the imagination. As children play with their cut-outs, they often see new possibilities. They can arrange and paste them onto coloured paper, or make them stand up by attaching a strip of light card (bent at right angles) to the back of figures. Cut-out figures can also become puppets (see Puppet People, page 99).

Pen and wash Pen drawings can be coloured with diluted food dye or watered-down tempera paint. Use fine brushes.

Wax resist This technique creates visual magic. It relies on the fact that oil resists water. Children draw firmly with crayons or oil pastels, then with soft brushes spread over the drawing a wash of diluted food dye, watered-down tempera paint or watercolour in one or more colours. Light crayon colours show up well against dark washes.

TIME AND SPACE FOR DRAWING

Drawing thrives when children can draw regularly and for as long as they like.

Children can draw at a table, on the floor, at easels, at a light table or on clipboards when outdoors. Even though drawing can take place practically anywhere, it's important that it has a 'home.' If at all possible, make a permanent space for drawing. Store drawing materials and scissors, stapler, sticky tape and paste in easily accessible separate containers.

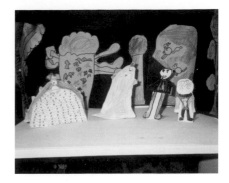

MATERIALS AND TOOLS

Begin with only a few materials – too much choice can be bewildering. But quality does matter: drawing with media that make strong clear marks is a happy and engaging experience. Select from the following:

Oil pastels, crayons Buy the thicker kinds as these are easier to hold and do not break readily. Both are suitable for very young children. Oil pastels have stronger colours than crayons and are softer in consistency, so less pressure is needed to make a mark.

Non-toxic water-based felt-tip pens These pens enable children to make clear precise marks. Offer very young children short thick pens in a few colours and make sure that they do not put pen caps in their mouths. Offer older children both thick and thin pens in black and a range of colours.

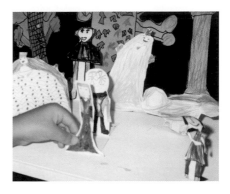

Cut-out drawings by five- and six-year-olds.

Chalk Use chalk on chalkboards and black or dark coloured paper.

Pencils Pencils are suitable for older experienced children. 2B pencils are best for general drawing. 3B, 4B and 6B pencils are softer and blacker. Coloured pencils are also useful.

Charcoal Charcoal provides an interesting change for experienced drawers. Good quality charcoal produces velvety marks. As charcoal sticks snap easily, break them into short pieces before giving them to children.

Paper Cartridge, litho, typing paper, brown paper, recycled office paper, black or dark paper (for use with chalks). Smooth surfaces (but not slippery) are best for felt tip pens. Paper with a slight tooth (texture) is better for crayons and pastels. Vary shapes and sizes so as to invite different kinds of drawings. A long roll of paper on the floor or across a table is useful for collaborative work.

A set-up for older children: pens stored in 'colour families'.

Miscellaneous Scissors with rounded tips, sticky tape, non-toxic paper paste or glue sticks, pencil sharpeners and clipboards for outdoor drawing. For older children include a stapler and hole punch.

SEE ALSO
Looking at Marks and Lines **16**
Bookmaking **97**
Sharing Interests and Passions **102**

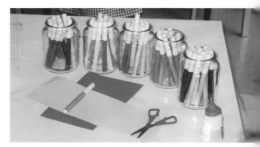

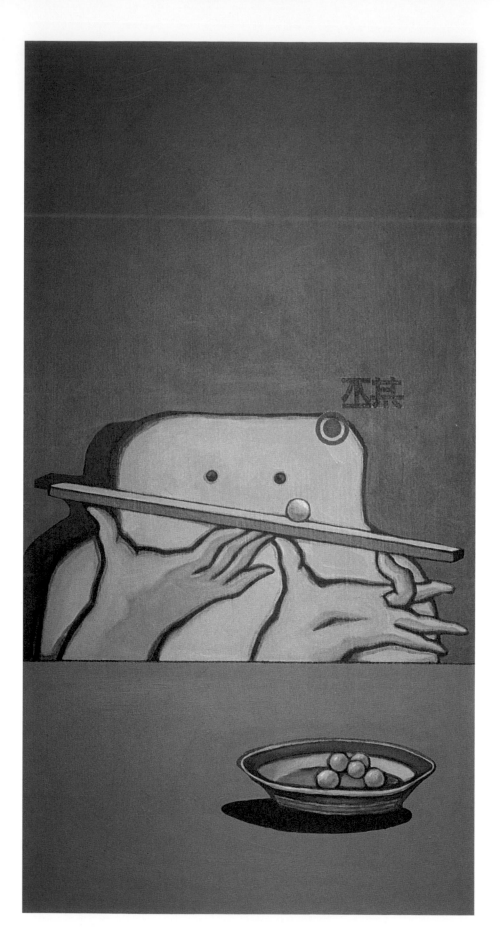

Funny yet serious, simple yet complex, this painting invites us to use our imagination. What story does it tell? Is it about the balancing acts we perform as we go through life? Is it perhaps about the delicate balance of all things in our universe? Or is it just about someone playing games? Which way will the ball roll?

Guan Wei (Chinese-born Australian)
Sliding Ball, 1991
Acrylic on canvas, 87 x 46 cm

Courtesy of the artist and
Sherman Galleries

Painting

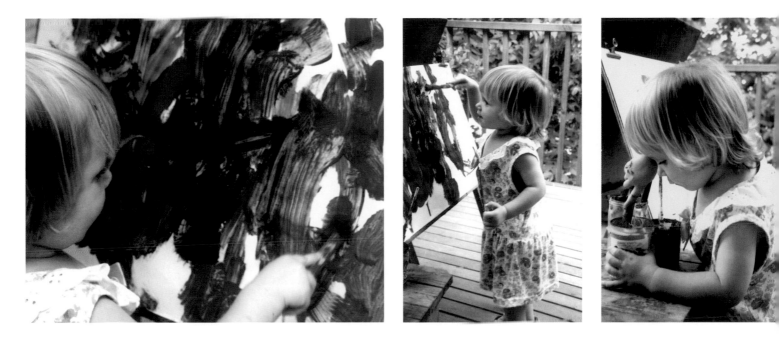

Painting is a wonderfully sensuous experience. Plunging into colour with a brush, gliding, swooping, skimming along, *changing* paper into a playspace aglow with colour – these are joys that enthral painters. In the rhythm and flow of painting the whole body is involved. Vision and movement intertwine. Painting is more, much more than making pictures. Being in a painting, becoming lost in it, is one way to describe the experience.

Compared to their drawings, children's paintings often show less detail. Partly this is because using a wide brush is very different from using a pen. But painting also fulfils other purposes. It involves a different kind of thinking. Painting can be about dividing a sheet of paper into rivers of colour and making colours sing.

Painting is another way of learning to see – similar to drawing but also very different.

Perhaps seeing things differently is why young children love 'painting' with clear water. Water will darken most surfaces – a surprise – and then magically evaporates – another surprise. Finger painting, a gentle, often mesmerising experience, also has wide appeal. However, although it is calming and beneficial, it offers less scope for exploring ideas than painting with a brush.

At times words are inadequate: a painting is about making visual magic. Enraptured by the surprise of colours appearing, changing and disappearing, a toddler adds layer upon layer of colour.

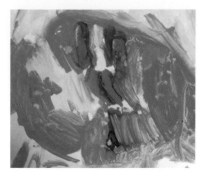

Covering an entire sheet of paper with areas of colour takes skill and concentration. This kind of painting fascinates many experienced children.

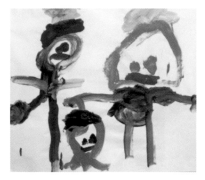

'My family' by a four-year-old. The figures stand proudly together as a family group on a 'ground line'.

APPRECIATING WHAT CHILDREN DO

At first very young children often paint just a patch of colour.

For beginners, learning how to get a brush out of the pot, onto the paper – and not somewhere else – and back into the *same* pot is often challenge enough. They may stick to one colour and ignore the rest – a beautiful blue by itself, for example, can be wondrous to a young toddler. On the other hand, some toddlers use three or more colours and manage most of the time to keep them separate.

Children realise early that a mark can stand for something. Initially they *find* meaning rather than set out deliberately to create it. 'Snail,' says Chris (23 months) pointing to a spiralling line that he's made by chance with his brush. It's one of those rare moments that allows an adult to witness how very young children *see meaning into* marks they've made. With one word Chris tells me he recognises the similarity between his marks and his memory of a snail's shell.

As with drawing, it's a special moment when children find they can make a line go around and return to its starting point. This enclosed shape can stand for anything. Gradually children add other lines and place smaller shapes inside it.

In time they begin to explore the entire painting space on the paper. They make short strokes, dots and irregular patches, often filling in spaces between marks. They discover how to make new colours by mixing, and many delight in creating separate areas of colour close to each other but not overlapping. Many make patterns by repeating marks in rows or in a circular fashion (see Discovering Patterns, page 33).

The shapes of human figures are similar to those in drawings, but they may be less detailed. Children know far more than they represent in their paintings, and often omit features if they have insufficient space on the paper. As children mature, their figures no longer appear isolated but in relationship to each other and to surroundings, such as houses and trees. They begin to use a line at the top of a painting to depict the sky and a line along the bottom to depict the ground.

- Share children's delight in what they've made *appear*. A smile, a nod, a glance of genuine interest may be all the acknowledgment they want. Four- year-old Aniella once taught me a valuable lesson. Looking up from the easel, she said with a broad smile and considerable insight: 'You like watching me, don't you?' I hadn't realized how much my silent gaze had pleased and sustained her in her efforts.

- Gently guide toddlers into returning brushes to the right pots of paint so that colours remain pure as long as possible. If several children want to paint, ensure that the next child has an equally enchanting experience, replacing paints and brushes with a clean set if necessary. It may seem a nuisance to clean up between children, but clean colours and clean brushes invite them to become engaged and to remain so for long periods. If children are upset about drips running down their paintings, show them how to wipe a brush across the edge of a paint pot so that excess paint drains into the pot.

- Encourage finger painters to explore what their fingers can do. What colours can they make?

- If children want comments, try affirming what they have done – for example, *I see you've made the blue change into green!* Alternatively, you might ask: *What's happening here – would you like to tell me?* Or comment on the amount of time spent. Depending on the particular child, five, ten, twenty minutes or longer of concentration is a considerable achievement. *You've spent a long time on this!* is a comment that pleases serious painters.

- *I want to paint a crocodile/fire engine but I don't know how – help me!* In this situation try to analyse with children what it is they want to do. It's very helpful to break down a task into steps. Which part would they like to start with first? The head? The body? The wheels? Sometimes looking at an actual example, pictures or a model may help.

- *I don't know what to paint!* A good answer to this plea is: *Try out the colours and see what the brush can do. Then, when you're ready to make a painting, you can have a fresh piece of paper.* You'll find that ideas invariably flow once a child interacts with paint in a relaxed manner.

Murals, banners and hangings Murals (large paintings), banners and hangings (paintings on cloth, usually suspended from a dowel rod) offer opportunities for children to work together on a large scale.

Will you be my friend? often seems to be an underlying theme when children work on murals in pairs and trios. Commenting on a mural (below), the children's teacher, Mary Mauger, remarked: 'This landscape mural was done by three friends. There are only two spaces at the easel so when I saw the three wanted to paint at the same time, I suggested they work on a large piece of paper together. They decided to paint what they could see through the glass door – our garden. After they had worked on it for three days, we left it to dry and to give them time to think about what to do next, if anything. The following week they painted in the worms beneath the foliage as we had found some in the garden and were studying them on a nearby table. As is often the case at this age, I find the issue of having and keeping friends a major underlying theme. What I mean is that the work is often secondary to the often unspoken questions: *Will you be my friend? Will you play with me?*'

Landscape by three four- to five-year-olds, acrylic paint.

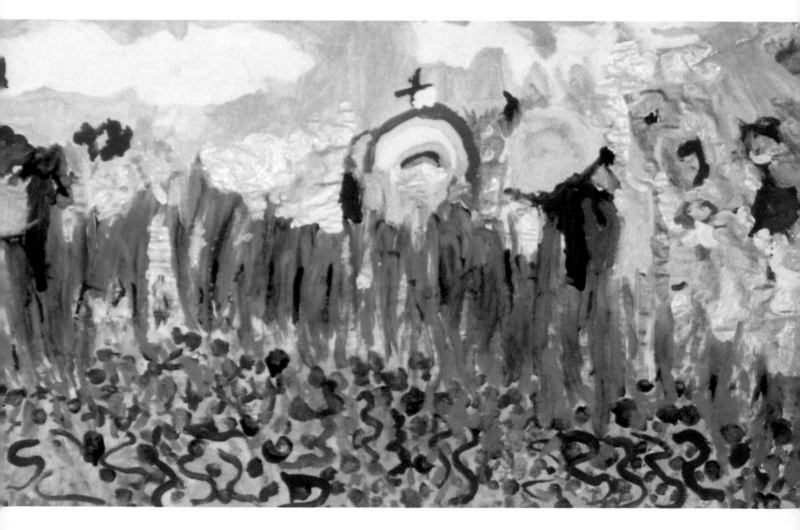

It is the children's third day on this mural. On the first day, two children painted the background in acrylic with rollers. The following day they painted sea animals (having studied these for several weeks). Now joined by a third child, they add details first in pencil and then in paint with fine brushes.

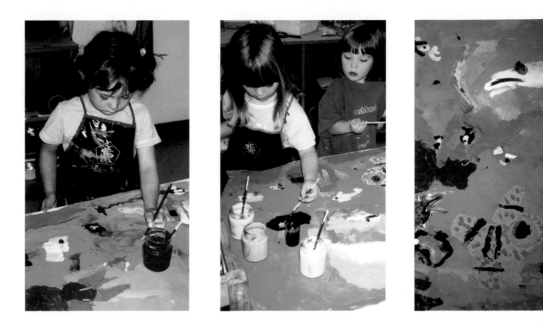

When a mural is the fruit of earlier explorations, it contains memories of things children have experienced and discovered. The following murals were done over several days after weeks of close observation, drawing and discussion.

Culminating a three-month-long investigation into the growth of seeds is the large mural below by four-year-olds. Their investigation began when they looked at a collection of seed pods brought in by a parent. Some of their early comments were: 'There's nuts inside', 'They are pips', 'You see pips in mandarins', 'They grow on the tree'. Over time, they studied germinating seeds, cut open various fruits to examine the seeds inside and decided, for instance, 'There's no pips in bananas'. They discussed and shared their findings through drawings and paintings, using felt-tip pens and watercolour paints to illustrate their theories about how seeds grow.

Sections from a mural depicting the growth of seeds by four-year-olds. Opaque and translucent paints and permanent markers on a sheet of clear plastic. Initially this sheet was laid on a table for children to draw on. At another session it was suspended against a window for them to continue working on it in paint with fine brushes.

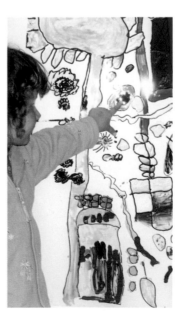

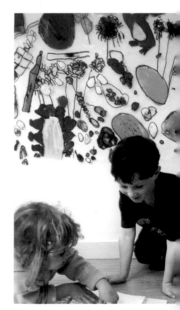

The starting point for the murals below was the children's intense interest in spirals. A ten-month-long learning adventure began when three children played with circles on an overhead projector, and one suggested that they try to make a spiral. They continued the next day and soon others became interested. Spirals became prevalent in their drawings and paintings, as well as claywork, collages, computer work and weaving. The children began to notice spirals in pinecones, shells, pineapples and other objects – not just at school, but at home and even during school holidays. Parents also became involved in the 'spiral research'.

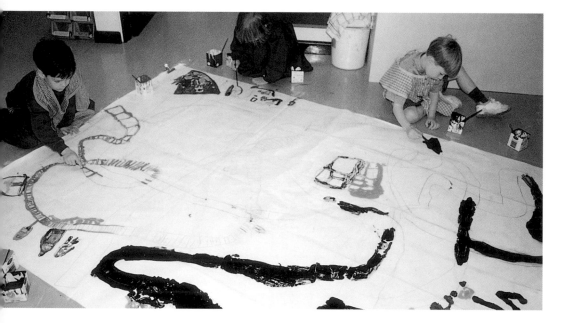

Four- and five-year-olds begin a large mural depicting spirals.

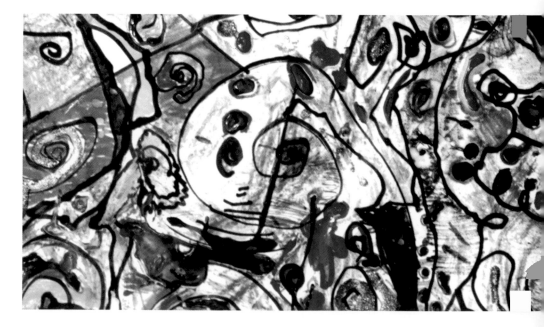

Detail from another mural: further ideas about spirals by four- and five-year-old children. Black felt-tip pen and food dye.

Using fine brushes and food dyes on a light table is another way to explore colour mixing.

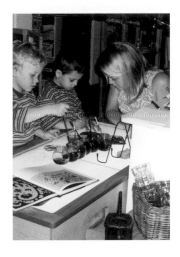

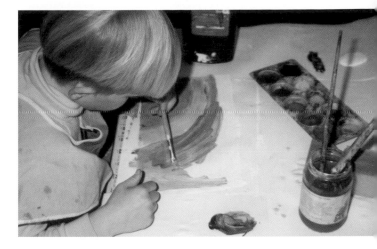

How many greys can you make? Engrossed in mixing 'cloud colours', a six-year-old makes many discoveries using white and black and a limited array of colours in a paint tray.

Colour mixing Watching colours blend, finding out that blue and yellow make green, yellow and red make orange, and red and blue make purple is part of the painting experience. However, children are capable of exploring colour mixing further. They delight, for instance, in the deliciousness of making pink (adding white to red), or the challenges of making a blue *lighter* (by adding white) or mixing a *bluer* purple or a *redder* purple. Whether children are interested in frogs or princesses doesn't matter: any topic can inspire investigations of colour.

Provide sheets of firm paper for mixing on, water for washing brushes, a sponge on which to dab excess water from brushes after rinsing, and several sheets of paper for painting.

Drawing and painting combined Children can colour their drawings with a wash of food dye, watered–down tempera or acrylic, using a fine brush (see Materials and Tools overleaf).

Mixed media Combine painting with paper collage. Provide paste paint (see page 130 for recipe) and a shallow tray of small pieces of paper beside the paints at the easel or painting table. You don't need paste for pasting collage papers as these adhere to the paste in the paint. Alternatively, children can paste pieces of paper on top of dry paintings using paste and brushes or glue sticks. Another combination is painting and printmaking.

Painting based on observational drawings Portrait drawings of friends and self–portraits (made with the use of mirrors) are good starting points for paintings. So are observational drawings of trees, flowers or animals (see Drawing from Observation, page 48).

TIME AND SPACE FOR PAINTING

Painting needs time – time for children to linger over a painting, and time to repeat experiences with familiar materials regularly. Some children complete a painting in a few minutes, others take half an hour.

Children can paint at child-sized easels either standing or sitting. (Toddlers tend to stay longer at an easel if they're able to sit while painting.) Painting at a table, a light table or on the floor are other options. Use plastic sheeting to protect floor and table surfaces. For some people aprons are a 'must', while others let children choose whether to wear them or not.

Position the painting set-up in a well-lit, quiet area, or in shade outdoors. Painting is often a contemplative experience and needs protection from the hurly-burly of other activities.

In school classrooms where large numbers of children are involved, it is wise to limit the number of painters and have only one painting station (perhaps six to twelve desks pushed together). Engage other children in alternative experiences, such as drawing.

Hang wet paintings on drying racks (e.g. clothes-drying racks). In classrooms cramped for space, you may have to use a line strung from the ceiling with clothes pegs or clips. If possible, write children's names on the backs of paintings rather than the front.

MATERIALS AND TOOLS

When buying paints, make sure they are labelled *non-toxic*. Whichever type you choose, paints should be a pleasure to use. Weak or muddy colours rarely engage children for long. The most common paints suitable for children are:

Tempera paint This produces bright opaque colour. It is available in powder and liquid form, and also in tubes or solid cakes. It comes in a variety of colours, plus black and white. Some tempera colours mixed together (e.g. blue and yellow) tend to make rather dull secondary colours. For this reason, it's a good idea to buy the secondary colours, green, orange and purple, as well as the three primary colours, red, yellow and blue. Get white and black too. Brown is also useful, although children can create a brown by mixing orange and black. In time you might get another blue and green, lighter or darker, to extend the range.

Tempera in liquid form can be used as it is. Pour it into a plastic paint container, mug or jar. Add a little water if it's very thick. Take care not to overfill the container. 2-3 cm of paint is sufficient.

To mix tempera powder with water, you need about two-thirds powder to one-third water. First pour a little water into a container and then add sufficient powder to make a paste. Gradually add more water to make a thin cream that allows a brush to glide easily.

When using use tempera paint in compressed form, wet the cake thoroughly with a soft brush dipped in water until it softens and produces the depth of colour desired. This takes some skill and practice, but older children enjoy the challenge.

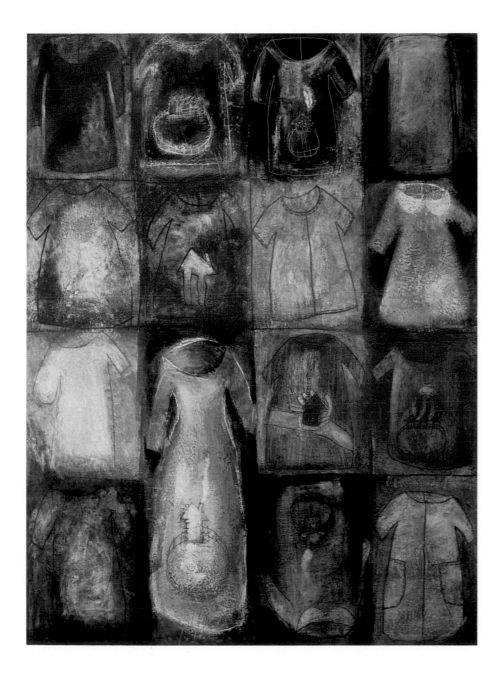

For me this painting's first attraction is its seductive colour and texture. I adore the glow of the colours and the rich surface (achieved by applying oil paint to layers of wax). But another attraction is the subject matter. What do these dresses stand for? There's no hint of a body in them, yet they seem filled with a human presence.

Sophie Gralton (Australian)
Beige Like Her Complexion, 2000
Oil and wax on canvas, 150 x 200 cm

Courtesy of the artist

Acrylic paint This produces bright opaque colour which can be made more transparent by adding water. It is available in liquid form and in tubes. Purchase the kinds labelled for kindergarten and school use. When dry, paintings can be painted over and other colours added.

Home-made paste paint This consists of a paste made with cornflour (cornstarch), coloured with vegetable dyes or food colouring. In contrast to the paints already described, this kind is translucent (see page 130 for a recipe).

Finger paint This can be purchased (labelled as finger paint), or you can simply make a thicker form of paste paint yourself. Spoon or pour a small amount directly onto a laminex table surface, or else put the paint in plastic ice cream containers on the table and let children spoon their own amounts. Aprons are essential. If you are working with children in a centre or school, place the table near a child-height sink as children's hands must be washed immediately they have finished. (Don't use buckets of water for washing hands as these have the potential to collect germs and become a source of cross-infection.) If at home but not near a sink, have a bucket of soapy water and paper towels handy.

To remove stains in clothes, soak them in cold water.

Paint containers For very young children, use mugs or plastic paint containers in a paint container holder. Many use paint containers with lids so that the paint can't spill. The drawback is that lids (either colourless or coloured) prevent children from looking at the paint inside the container – something very young children love to do. If a coloured lid doesn't match the colour inside, as sometimes happens, the set-up is confusing. Having watched two-year-olds competently use lidless containers, I'm convinced that lids are unnecessary provided that the containers are in a holder.

Provide experienced children with paint in plastic paint trays or egg cartons.

How many colours? My answer is simply this: observe the children and take your cues from them. Gradually increase the range of colours – anything from three to eight or even more – *according to children's preferences and abilities to handle a wide range*. From time to time try also limiting the range (providing only black and grey, for example). In this way you add interest and complexity.

Extending the colour range Try extending the range of bought colours. For example, to make pastel colours, begin with white and add a small amount of the desired colour. Stir with a paintbrush.

To mix pink, add a small amount of red to white paint. To obtain a deeper pink, add more red. Bright vermilion and orangey-reds will give you warm pinks (because they contain yellow), while deeper reds, crimsons and burgundy-reds produce cooler pinks (because they contain a small amount of blue). To make a lilac-tinted pink, add a trace of blue or purple. Strong, strident pinks such as 'hot pink' are difficult to make, so it's best to buy a ready-made fluorescent pink. Mix bought fluorescent pink with white to obtain pastel tints.

To make colours darker, add a tiny amount of black.

Paper Firm paper, such as cartridge or litho paper, is ideal. Newsprint is cheaper but soaks up paint, dulls colours and tears easily. The back of used paper from architectural drafting offices provides good surfaces.

The colour of paper affects the colours used on top. For example, a dark blue sheet makes transparent and semi-transparent paints appear darker and/or duller. Yellow paint on a blue sheet may seem greenish. To make colours stand out on black or dark colours, add white to the paint.

The size and shape of paper influences what children do, so try offering different sizes and shapes.

Brushes Quality and size really do matter. Although good brushes cost more, they are worth buying. A good brush springs back into shape, does not shed hairs and holds paint well. It lasts longer than a poor brush and offers a wonderfully sensuous experience. Poor brushes shed hairs, become limp and can take all the joy out of painting.

The size and width of brushes influence children. A wide brush encourages them to paint patches and glorious swathes of colour, while a narrow one leads to more precise, detailed work. Medium-sized brushes are the most practical to buy initially, but gradually try to acquire others. Buy short-handled brushes for toddlers. Use sturdy brushes for 'water' painting on fences, concrete and other rough surfaces.

For painting on large sheets, wide and medium bristle, nylon or hogs hair brushes are useful. For painting on small sheets, offer fine nylon brushes. A change in brush size can do wonders to renew a child's interest in painting.

Provide one brush per colour. Supply experienced children with jars of water for rinsing their brushes (and a sponge pad for dabbing away excess water).

Taking care of brushes Always clean brushes thoroughly with water immediately after use; if this isn't possible, soak them in water immediately. Store them with bristles upright (the other way ruins them). Occasionally you may need to remind children to handle brushes with care.

Alternatives to brushes? Some books suggest using novel implements for painting, such as dishmops, string, drinking straws, balloons, marbles, and even spoons. Unfortunately these rarely encourage creativity. It's difficult for children to control such implements or develop skills with them. Attempting to make meaningful marks with a spoon is a bit like trying to dance in boots three sizes too big.

An exception is the humble cotton bud. Used with food dye, cotton buds enable young children to make fine lines which they find fascinating. When children are around four years of age, however, fine brushes generally offer them more scope.

Rollers are useful for covering a large sheet of paper with acrylic paint. Once it is dry, children can paint details with brushes.

SEE ALSO
Discovering Shapes **18**
Discovering Colours **26**
Discovering Textures **31**
Discovering Patterns **33**
Printmaking **91**

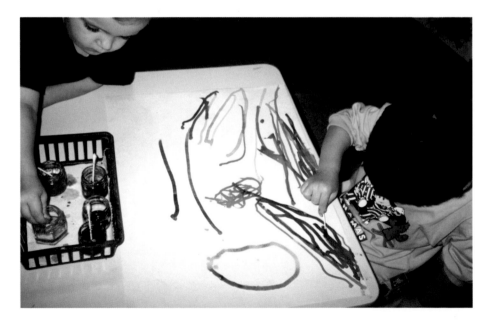

Young three-year-olds delight in making fine lines and circular shapes with cotton buds dipped in food dye.

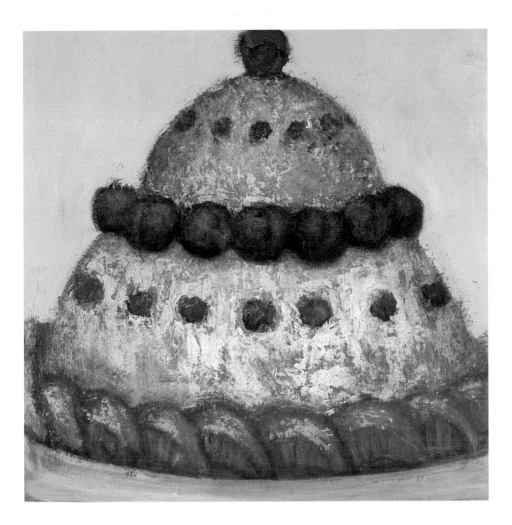

Resplendent as a fairytale palace, this monumental cake rests majestically on its plate. I chose this painting partly because cakes are important to young children – from an early age they know cakes play a special role in birthday celebrations and family rituals. But I also chose it for its sense of fun and fantasy, and for the deliciousness of its colour and texture.

Kate Dorrough (Australian)
Crème à l'Orange, 2001
Oil and acrylic on board, 60 x 60 cm

Courtesy of the artist

Claywork

Clay invites touching and squeezing. A wonderfully malleable material, it is fascinating in its own right. Young children love to speculate on its origins. To my question, 'What can you tell me about clay?' a trio responded with: 'It comes from under the ground'; 'It's sort of mud'; 'You buy it in a shop'.

I believe it's crucial that children have contact with this basic elemental material that has been used by humans for thousands of years. Formed from the weathering of rocks, clay can range in colour from white, grey and ochre to reddish brown, pale brown, dark brown and dark grey.

Claywork can be a language for exploring and communicating ideas. Like drawing, claywork enables children to make their ideas visible – but in three dimensions. It can be an exciting experience for young children to discover that they have made something with a 'back' and 'sides' as well as a 'front', and even an 'inside' and an 'underneath'.

Clay or dough? Dough and clay are both valuable, but they serve different purposes and different age-groups (see Discovering Forms, page 21).

Clay allows children to work on both a bigger and smaller scale than they can with dough. With clay they can make large, firm, complex structures as well as intricate details. They can also work on pieces over days provided you keep them moist with a plastic covering. When pieces are finished, simply let them dry out on a shelf (clay hardens when exposed to air). If you want a permanent finish, they can be fired in a kiln.

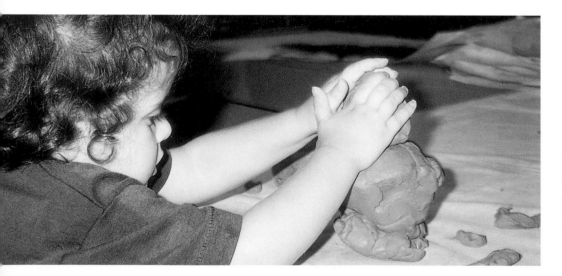

Balancing pieces on top of each other, a two-year old discovers fascinating possibilities.

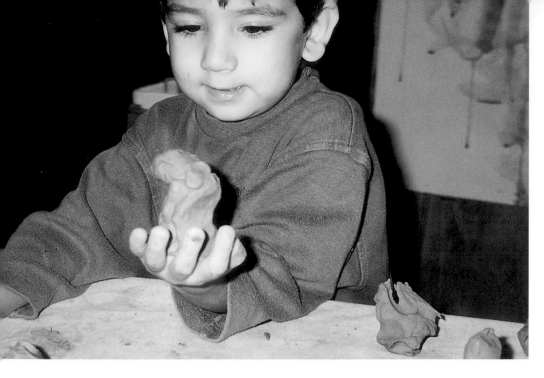

'Look! He's standing!'
Making something that can
stand is one the joys of
working with clay.

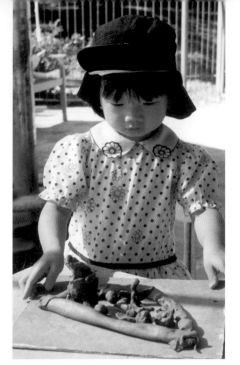

A three-year-old delights in
her 'family'.

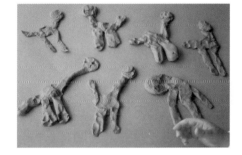

'Dinosaurs' by a four-year-old,
made one after the other.

APPRECIATING WHAT CHILDREN DO

By 22 to 24 months of age children may delight in touching clay, or at least watching others manipulate it. They are more likely to touch it if they've already had experience with dough. (Yet it's best to wait until children are past putting dough or clay in their mouths.)

Toddlers (and older children experiencing clay for the first time) begin by patting, stroking, squashing, pinching, squeezing, poking holes, breaking bits off and amassing pieces of clay on top of each other. Ideas emerge, grow and change as you watch. Often you get a step-by-step commentary, like this one from Joel (3 years 1 month): 'It's got a tail here. It's got a head here. It goes through the tunnel' (as he pushes a lump through an arched piece). 'Yes. That's it. It's a dog. It's a dalmatian!'

Children gradually learn how to roll balls and coils (see Claywork Terms, page 70). They practise these skills constantly.

Some children create stories while animating lumps of clay; others prefer to make careful arrangements of clay pieces, and yet others enjoy piling pieces on top of each other.

In time children begin to make human figures. To overcome the difficulty of representing individual body parts, they may simply tell you what various parts of a lump are meant to stand for. Learning how to join pieces of clay together is a skill that needs much practice.

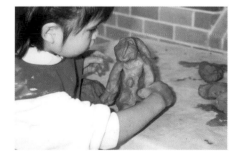

Learning to join pieces firmly
together takes practice.

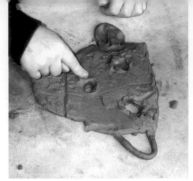
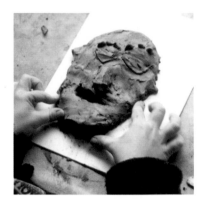

Masks by five-year-olds.

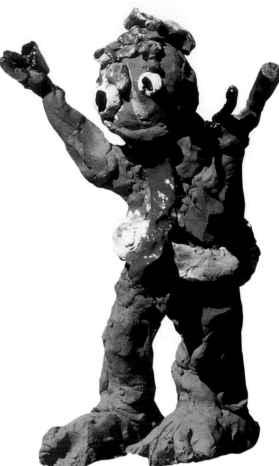

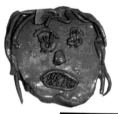

Portrait of a friend (based on a drawing).

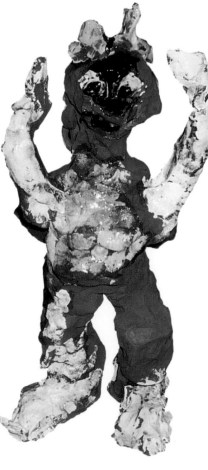

'Dancers'. The figures are approximately 40 cm high and have been fired, glazed and then fired a second time. Each was made by three four-year-olds in stages over a period of time. They belong to a series of figures made by children inspired by watching dancers in performance.

Experienced children are able to work together on structures. The photographs tell the story of one such structure, which the children named 'Rapunzel's Supermarket'. Four girls worked on this, and for over an hour they attempted to save it from collapse. Each child brought different skills to the group. As their building kept on collapsing, they had to keep on finding creative solutions. But as experienced clay builders with a shared understanding of clay, they were able to work deftly.

To some, working on a collapsing structure may seem unproductive. But when you realise how much the children learnt about structure and balance, and about sharing and accepting each other's ideas, their real achievement becomes apparent.

The rescue of 'Rapunzel's Supermarket', a clay structure on the verge of collapse. For over an hour the children explored various solutions. (Their ages ranged from 4 years 9 months to 5 years 1 month.)

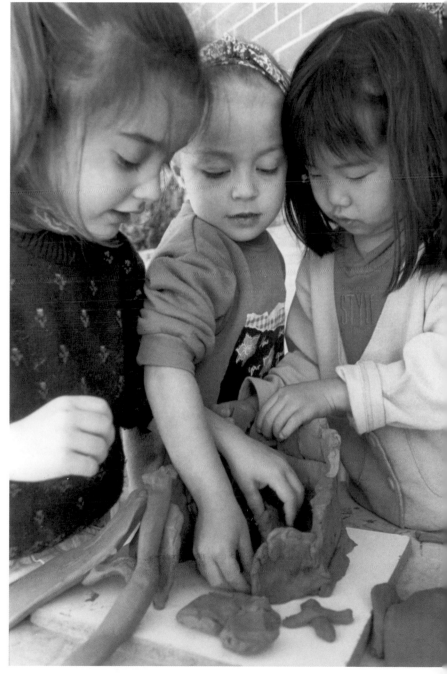

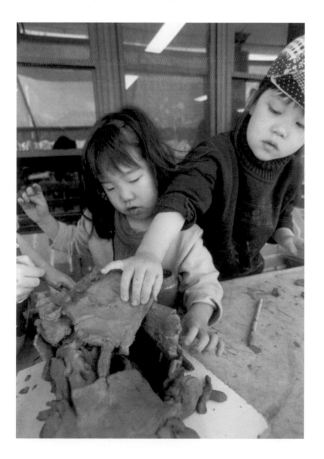

CLAYWORK TERMS

armature: internal support used by sculptors to hold up a structure.

coil: a potter's term for a rolled length of clay.

earthenware: type of clay, either white or brown. Recommended for children's use.

glaze: shiny surface on ceramic objects obtained by applying glazing material after first firing. Objects are then fired a second time.

kiln: special oven for firing clay objects. Operates at very high temperatures.

slab: piece of clay rolled flat with a rolling pin and cut to shape.

slip: mixture of clay and water used as a decorating medium by potters.

slurry: similar to slip but contains less water. Used as a paste for joining pieces.

stoneware: type of clay which is fired at a higher temperature than earthenware.

terracotta: type of clay, always brown. Recommended for children's use.

wedging: vigorous banging and kneading of clay to expel air. Necessary if clay is to be fired, as the presence of air may cause an explosion. A new packet of clay, however, is usually free of air bubbles.

INTERACTING AND GUIDING

- A good way to begin is to offer each child a grapefruit-sized amount of clay divided into two or three pieces. Very young children may prefer a number of small pieces – to some a large lump seems daunting, and at first they may only wish to pat small bits.

- Even if you don't care for clay yourself, show children that you feel positively about it. For example, knead the clay or roll some coils or build a column. In this way you alert children to interesting possibilities. Try not to flatten the clay into pancake-like pieces because this tends to limit children's thinking. Resist the temptation to make something specific, like an animal, because children may stop working and beg you to make more things for them.

- Try to avoid asking *What is it?* as this assumes claywork has to 'be' something. Often there is no need to say anything – children may only want you to watch sympathetically. If they want a response to their work, comment on their achievements – for example, *I see you've made yours stand up/ you've joined your pieces carefully.* This helps them to focus on what they've achieved and gives them confidence to continue.

- Remember that it takes time for children to learn to make things stand up. Being subject to gravity, clay forbids flights of fancy and structures often collapse. So be ready to give help: for example, *Shall I hold your elephant while you put on its trunk?*

- Show children techniques when it seems they have a use for them. For instance, when Sue wanted to make a roof for a clay house, it was a good moment to show her how to make a *slab* of clay. Similarly, show children how to join clay when the need arises (see Further Challenges opposite).

- Talk things through with children who need help in starting. For instance, to a child wanting to make a crocodile, you might say: *Tell me what you know about crocodiles.* Any part of a crocodile named by the child – whether head, body, or even the tail – can be a starting point.

- Remind experienced children to join pieces firmly and to avoid making them paper-thin, as these will crumble when dry. Invite children to collaborate on a large piece or several related pieces. Help them to set themselves a goal and work out how they might start.

- Encourage children to help each other. Experienced clay builders are often generous in giving assistance. For instance, Lina (4 years 2 months, with two years experience) gave this advice to Ben when his sculpture threatened to topple: 'You put something under it so it can stand up. Put another like this piece. Yes, yes! Stick this right on. See? It's standing, it's standing!'

It takes practice to roll what potters call 'coils'. Coils can be used in many ways. When children master this skill, they become more able to use clay as a means for representing ideas.

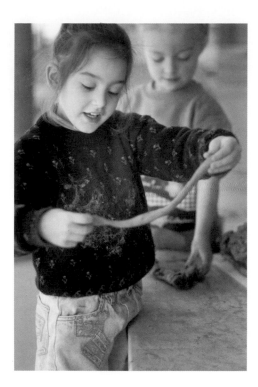

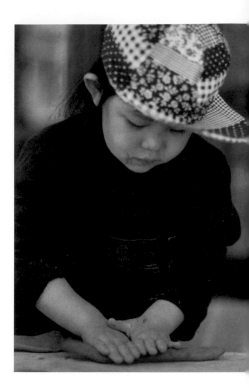

FURTHER CHALLENGES

Below are some clay techniques that are useful when children want to make more complex structures. Don't feel you have to be an expert to use them. It's far more helpful for children if you think of yourself as a fellow learner. Be experimental in your approach: for instance, you might say, *Let's see if this will work. If it doesn't, we'll try something else.*

Coils Rolling coils is a skill that requires practice. Make a few and then let children take over. It's important to use the full length of your fingers; coils tend to break if you only use the pads of the fingers. Work from the middle of the coil outwards.

Slabs A slab is a flat rectangular or square piece of clay which lends itself to all sorts of uses. Roll clay to between 1/2 and 1cm thick and slice it into tiles (rectangular, square, circular, oval or irregular shapes). If the clay sticks to your working surface, roll the slab on a piece of paper.

Children can use slabs of clay like building blocks.

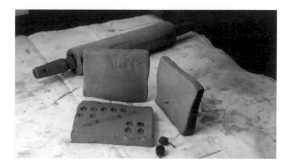

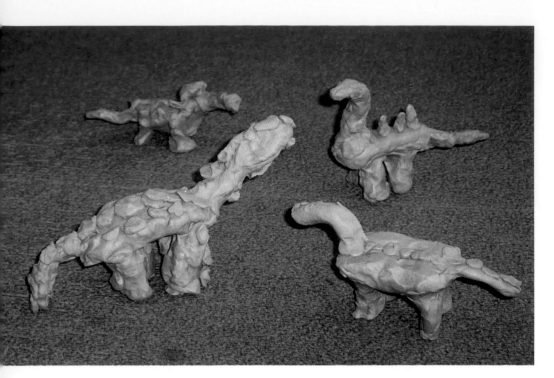

Each of these 'dinosaurs' is supported by an internal armature.

Armatures When children begin to make upright structures such as 'trees', their early attempts frequently collapse. To make a structure stand, insert a paddle-pop stick or piece of dowelling as an armature down the middle of a piece of clay and make a supporting base. Remember that items containing wooden armatures cannot be fired in a kiln.

Slurry Slurry is a paste used for joining pieces. To make some, dissolve clay into an equal quantity of water to make a thick cream. Apply with a narrow brush.

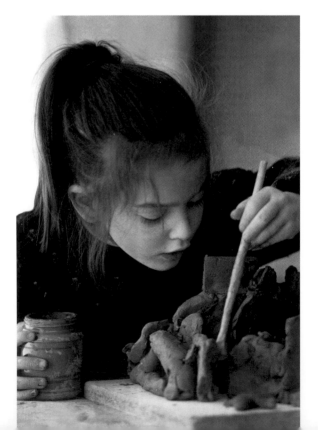

A child applies slurry before joining pieces together.

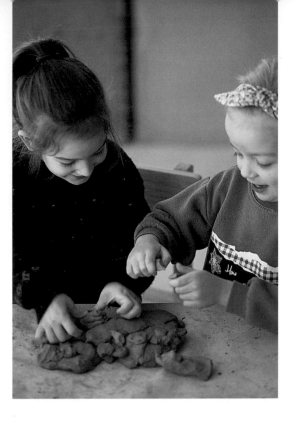

A clay table is a special place for sharing discoveries.

Making textures Make impressions by pressing finger tips, knuckles, or found objects (e.g. seedpods) into clay. Pinch it to make protruding ridges. Or dip a finger in slurry and rub it over the surface till it's smooth and shiny.

Making pots Children often discover how to make pots themselves by using the following ancient pinch-pot method. Hold a ball of clay in both hands cupped together; insert both thumbs simultaneously in the middle and then gradually part the thumbs, one to each side. Continue hollowing out the ball with thumb and fingers.

However, a word of caution: if pottery is introduced too early, children tend to think 'making pots' is what claywork is all about. They may then miss out on the joys and stimulation of using clay for exploring ideas.

TIME AND SPACE FOR CLAYWORK

A clay table is a special space for sharing discoveries. It can be placed indoors or out. For a description of an outdoor space for claywork that functioned like a studio, see page 114.

Try to have clay available as often as possible, and for as long as possible. It takes time for children to get used to working with it and to develop skills.

An ideal working surface is a table covered with heavy-duty artists' canvas cloth (obtainable from artists' suppliers). This is expensive but lasts indefinitely and provides a neutral absorbent surface that is excellent to work on. To clean the cloth, hose it down. Alternatively, use wooden boards or plain lino pieces on a table covered with a plain plastic cloth. If working indoors, you may need to cover the floor with plastic.

Clay You can buy terracotta or earthenware clay in bags (generally 10 to 12 kilos) from artists', potters' or kindergarten suppliers. It is inexpensive, especially considering that it can be used indefinitely (provided no foreign materials like leaves are imbedded in it). One bag will go far with a group of children, but as they begin to save their items and work on a bigger scale, you will need several.

Clay must be soft and malleable. This is vital. Clay that's hard or very sticky is unpleasant to use.

Clay cutter To cut a block of clay you will need a cutter. Use 30 cm of fishing line with a button attached at each end.

Boards Assorted firm cardboard or wooden boards for supporting work are useful.

Aprons Aprons are useful, but don't fuss if children refuse to wear them.

Additional items For more experienced children provide paddle-pop sticks and pieces of dowelling. Use these as armatures. The sticks are also useful for cutting and trimming slabs.

An adult-size rolling pin (children's rolling pins have insufficient weight).

Plastic jars with lids, or mugs, for slurry, and narrow brushes to apply it.

Oddments for adding texture to clay (e.g. seedpods, shells, cotton reels).

A roll of plastic wrap for covering ongoing work so that it remains damp. In hot weather, cover work with a damp cloth, then heavy-duty plastic.

Kiln It's not necessary to fire claywork in a kiln. The examples shown in the photographs (unless otherwise stated) were simply placed on a shelf to dry and remained unfired. However, when children make complex pieces you may like to consider firing them. Objects must be completely dry before firing. Note that clay can explode during firing for several reasons: presence of moisture, pockets of air or foreign bodies. If you want to use a kiln, you need to ensure that pieces stand a good chance of surviving the firing. The clay should not exceed 1 cm in thickness.

CARING FOR CLAY

Clay must be kept moist. When it's been worked for an extended period, its moisture evaporates and must be replaced. Encourage children to help you in the following steps:

- After use, roll clay into grapefruit-sized balls.

- Make a thumb hole in each ball and fill it with water. (A doll's jug is useful for this.) Use more or less water depending on the condition of the clay. Store in an airtight container in a cool place.

Recycling Recycling is necessary when hardened pieces accumulate.

- Collect completely dry pieces in a plastic tub or basin. Remove any leaves, dirt, etc.

- Traditionally the next step is to hammer the dry clay into small pieces. While this quickens the softening, clay dust can be a health hazard when a large quantity is crushed, so consider omitting this step.

- Pour sufficient water over the pieces (crushed or uncrushed) to cover them.

- When all pieces have softened (which may take hours for crushed clay or days for uncrushed), tip out any excess water and leave uncovered for more hours/days.

- When the mixture is no longer liquid (usually after a few days), scoop it out onto a canvas cloth or board.

- When it's no longer sticky, roll it into balls and store them in an air-tight container.

- When washing tools, note that clay lumps may clog the sink.

HEALTH AND SAFETY

Avoid inhaling the dust formed when dry pieces of clay crumble. Remove it with a vacuum cleaner, damp cloth or damp sponge, not a broom or brush.

Do all recycling outside so that clay dust does not accumulate in confined spaces. Protect your eyes if hammering clay. If you decide to hammer a large amount, it's advisable not to have children present. Wear an inexpensive nose and mouth mask (obtainable from chemists).

SEE ALSO
Discovering Forms **21**
Discovering Textures **31**
Sharing Ideas and Passions **102**

Collage

The word *collage* comes from the French word *coller*, meaning to paste. A collage is a pasted arrangement of papers and other materials on a flat surface.

When materials speak to the imagination, interesting things can happen. For instance, when four-year-olds Natalie and Rani rummaged through a basket of left-over paper pieces, Natalie found a torn piece which reminded her of a shaggy dog. Waving the scrap in the air, she made it 'bark'. Rani was enchanted. With Rani's attention egging her on, Natalie then pasted the scrap onto a large sheet of paper and drew a pair of eyes on it. Deciding the dog needed a leash, she drew one on it and then added the dog's owner: a girl named Goldilocks. Meanwhile Rani pasted pieces of coloured paper onto the sheet. And so the two continued, creating an ever richer concoction of collage, drawing and story.

APPRECIATING WHAT CHILDREN DO

Paste fascinates young children. If left to their own devices, they may apply copious amounts to a sheet without actually pasting anything on it. When they manage to paste pieces onto a sheet, they often layer them, one on top of the other in a patch.

Sticky tape also intrigues young children, and two- and three-year-olds may tirelessly practise their skills in using it. It can be an eye-opening experience to watch experienced under-threes at work with paper and sticky tape. They delight in using bits of paper to cover and uncover, hide and reveal. What you see in the end often conceals the experiments they have made.

The speed of young children's actions, their utter determination to master skills almost beyond their abilities, and the startling ease with which they can transform bits of paper, makes you realise how much they can accomplish when materials and conditions are 'just right'.

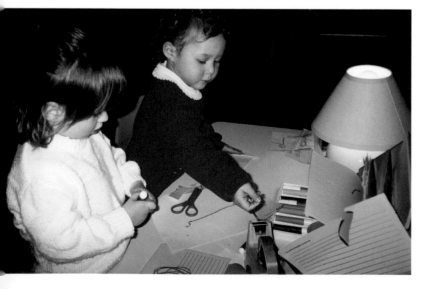

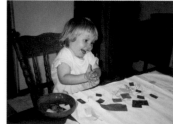

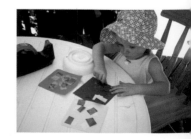

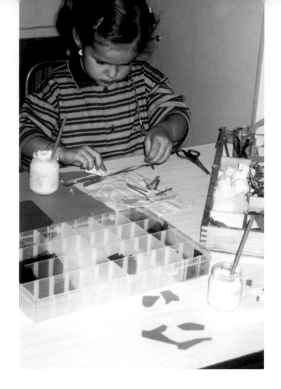

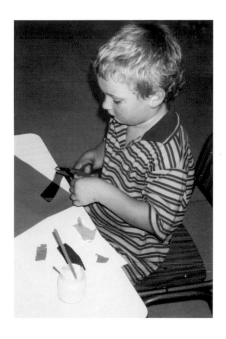

Cutting requires much practice. Children often enjoy simply snipping and cutting for its own sake. Gradually they begin to organise and arrange their cut bits and pieces. As with drawing and painting, pattern-making may become evident (see also Discovering Patterns, page 33).

Experienced children may combine collage pieces with drawing to make recognisable pictures. They may also use paper three-dimensionally so that pieces project or fold out from the surface.

INTERACTING AND GUIDING

■ Help children to develop pasting skills. For example, show them how to use less paste by wiping the brush on the edge of the container. Remind them to work slowly. In general, I'd be inclined to wait until children are nearly two or older before introducing collage.

■ Look at materials with the children. Encourage them to spend time choosing. 'It looks like fingers' was John's response to a left-over scrap with dangling ends. The 'fingers' inspired him to make a paper giant.

■ Comment on features in children's work: *I see you've pasted those pieces all in a row*.

■ Help children to use scissors and remind them to be careful. It may take a long time before they manage to make some snips. You can help by holding the sheet for them. Light card is often easier to snip than paper.

■ Add items in response to children's interests and emerging stories. On the other hand, don't be afraid to offer only one kind of paper or a narrow range of colours for fear of limiting creativity. As long as materials are open-ended and contain a number of possibilities, constraints can often encourage creativity. For instance, when Jenny and Sarah had tissue paper and cellophane

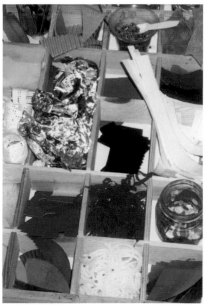

Choosing, cutting and pasting enticing materials is an absorbing experience. Choosing is in itself a creative act.

77

in only one colour (blue), they found they could make all kinds of blueness by overlapping pieces. This was something they had never done before.

- Sometimes you might introduce a technique to trigger new ideas, but avoid techniques that are simply for 'effect'. For example, pasting twisted bits of tissue paper is boring and offers little to the imagination, unless it is something children have discovered for themselves.

FURTHER CHALLENGES

Here are some ways children can transform pieces of paper before pasting them.

Tearing Tearing out a shape – as opposed to ripping paper – is actually difficult to do. If you show children how to tear a piece of paper very, *very* slowly, some may try their hand at it. Different types of paper all tear differently, and it makes a difference whether you tear along the grain or against it (try this out with newspaper). Tissue paper 'asks' to be torn as it is difficult for children to cut.

Cut-out drawings Experienced cutters might cut out their drawings (or photocopies of drawings). This takes practice and you may need to help. Children can paste cut-outs onto contrasting coloured backgrounds, or make them into puppets (see Puppet People on page 99).

Doors and windows To make a 'door' or 'window' in a sheet of paper, draw a rectangular shape. Cut along three sides of the rectangle and fold along the fourth. This creates a door or window that opens and shuts.

Mixed media A basket of pre-cut papers beside a tray of paints can inspire children to combine collage with painting. There is no need to provide paste because acrylic paint or paint made with cornflour (cornstarch) paste acts as a glue.

Three-dimensional collage Paper shapes can project from the background. Invite children to think of ways of making paper shapes stand up.

See-through shapes Tear or cut out a shape in a continuous movement. You will then have both a 'positive' shape and also an empty space of the same shape, a 'negative' shape or, to use a term I use with children, a 'see-through' shape. Draw their attention to a negative shape by placing a contrasting colour under it so that another colour appears in the space. Five- to six-year-olds may see interesting possibilities.

Crowns and head-dresses Children can design and make headgear using lengths of firm paper or light card, approximately 12 x 60 cm. They can cut zigzag and other shapes along the edge. They can also draw or paint patterns on it or decorate it with collage materials. Staple the card into a band to fit around the head.

Figuring out how to transform a flat piece of paper into a wearable object delights experienced children.

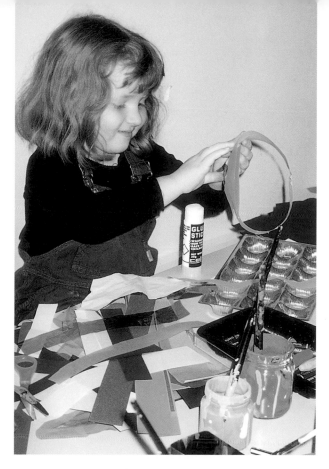

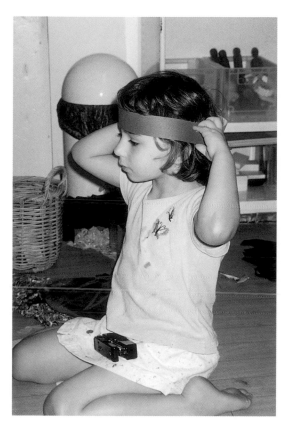

Will it fit? Experienced children like solving this problem for themselves.

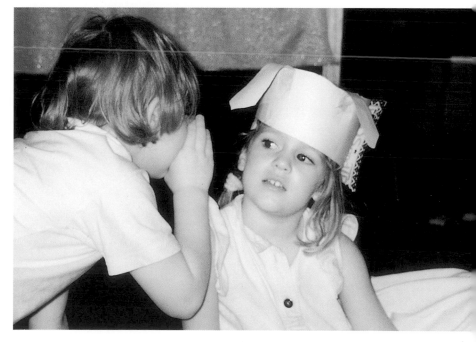

Complete with floppy ears, this crown is for a 'Rabbit Princess' – a good example of the imaginative approach children adopt when free to design their own head-dresses.

Allow children plenty of time to explore familiar materials and to practise pasting and cutting skills.

All you need is table-space and a chair for each child, and a choice of appealing materials. Begin with a small selection of papers. Think of the materials as a *palette* of colours, textures and shapes. An attractive display encourages children to choose carefully. However, it's easy to go overboard; remember that a vast array of items makes it difficult for children to become focused.

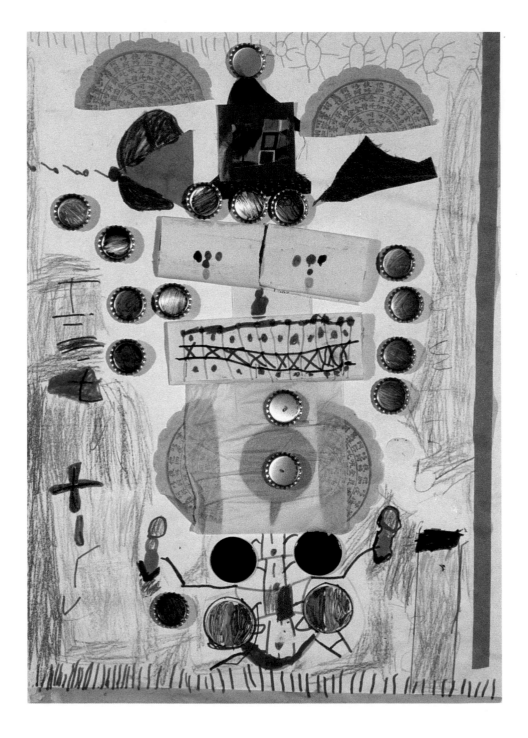

This collage shows a strong feeling for pattern and symmetry. It was made by two four-year-old boys working side by side at an easel. It's interesting to see how they have combined various materials with drawing.

Place materials invitingly in shallow baskets or plastic containers (preferably white or clear so that children can see the materials easily). If possible, place the containers on a nearby shelf or second table, so that the working surface is left uncluttered.

Paper Paper is the most flexible material for young children. They can tear, cut, paste, fold or scrunch it, draw on it, punch holes in it or make it stand up. With ease they can transform a piece of paper into a person – or a monster. Only paper paste or sticky tape need be used. Choose paper that is easy to tear, cut and paste. For children who are not yet proficient with scissors, provide small pieces in irregular or geometric shapes. Avoid realistic shapes as adult-made shapes can limit children's imagination. Left-over cut and torn scraps as well as paper strips are useful too.

Depending on children's levels of experience, gradually offer other types of paper as ideas develop. Sort pieces according to colour or texture, or contrasting qualities such as: shiny/dull; transparent/translucent/opaque; patterned/plain; light/dark; rough/smooth.

Solid colours Coloured paper (matt and glossy) in packs of squares or rectangles in a range of sizes – obtainable from artists' and school suppliers and newsagents – is easy to tear, cut and paste. Packs contain a variety of colours and usually black as well. Black is important for contrast. Brown paper is also useful.

Translucent colours Tissue paper is difficult to cut with children's scissors, but easy to tear. Colours become translucent particularly when pasted onto translucent or transparent surfaces (see Bases below). The colours of some brands may run when wet. Variations of colour are formed when pieces overlap each other. Use with diluted white PVA glue (see Adhesives overleaf).

Food for the eye: appealing materials invite a thoughtful response.

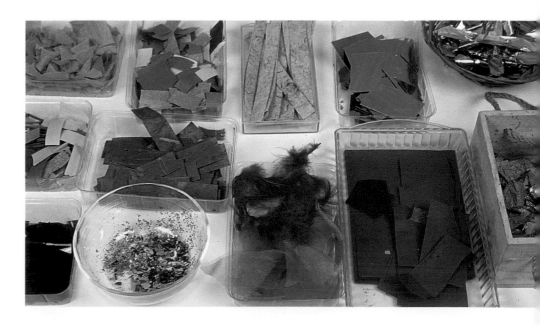

Transparent colours Cellophane produces brilliant transparent colour, particularly on transparent or translucent surfaces, and is also effective on white paper. It is useful for exploring colour as well as light. Since it's difficult to cut or tear, offer it in small pieces.

Shiny paper Foil, metallic paper, and chocolate wrappers appeal to the imagination. Chocolate wrappers are an excellent source for jewel-like colours.

Textured paper Light corrugated card found in packaging or purchased in rolls, paper doilies and wallpapers from discontinued sample books provide a range of textures.

Patterned paper Giftwrap and wallpaper pieces with tiny all-over patterns.

Other materials As children become experienced other materials can be offered, a few at a time. Most materials other than paper need a glue stronger than paper paste (see Adhesives opposite). They also require more patient handling.

Soft items Small pieces of plain and patterned fabrics, felt, lace, net, ribbon, yarns, wools and leather scraps.

Wood items Wood shavings (make sure these are dust-free), matchsticks manufactured for craft activities and paddle-pop sticks obtainable in bulk from craft shops and newsagents.

Plastic and metal items Lids and bottle tops in various sizes.

Found natural materials Collect sufficient quantities in perhaps three or four contrasting shapes: for example, fine twigs, gumnuts, broad flat leaves and slivers of bark. Children need patience and good pasting skills to work with these materials as they rarely have flat surfaces. It can be helpful for children to work together on a single base. Alternatively, small bases (A4 size) ensure that less patient children don't lose interest too quickly. Many natural materials may be better left unglued because glue can spoil their appearance. For an alternative, see page 35.

Things to avoid Avoid objects small enough to be swallowed and fiddly items like confetti that can be frustrating to handle and difficult to arrange for inexperienced children. Also avoid ready-made images. Although magazines, catalogues and used greeting cards are fine for a cutting spree, they have limited potential for children's own image-making. It's rare for young children to use ready-made images with the degree of creativity they show in their own drawings.

Bases (backgrounds) Bases must be firm enough to withstand the weight of materials. Vary shapes, sizes and colours as these influence children's thinking; familiar materials look new when pasted onto different bases.

Use firm paper such as cartridge, light card (white and coloured), backs of calendars, recycled office paper, large envelopes, paper bags and shoe box lids.

Large sheets of paper, architectural drafting paper or acetate placed on top of a light table (a table with translucent top and lights underneath) are useful for group work. Acetate requires PVA glue (see below).

Adhesives For young children, provide bought non-toxic paper paste or make paste with cornflour (cornstarch) – see page 130 for a recipe. Older children can use non-toxic roll-on glue sticks for paper work.

Sticky tape in a heavy-duty dispenser, or pre-cut in strips stuck along on the rim of a plastic plate, is useful; two to three year-olds often work more creatively with sticky tape than they can with paste. Sticky tape, however, can detract from the appearance of a work and is expensive when used in large quantities.

Non-paper items require stronger glue. Use non-toxic white PVA woodworking glue, which dries clear. For economy, dilute it with a little water and pour small amounts into shallow containers. Sponges for wiping off excess glue are useful. Provide paper towels for wiping hands.

Tools Paste brushes or paddle-pop sticks for applying paste or glue. Wash brushes thoroughly in water after use. Child-size scissors with rounded ends (make sure they really cut). Felt-tip pens, oil pastels, crayons or pencils for adding details. Stapler and hole-punch for older children (optional).

Building and Construction

The urge to build and construct with whatever materials are at hand begins early. Toddlers make nests for themselves out of cushions, while older children tirelessly construct cubby houses.

It's fascinating to see how often the house image crops up in things children make. This isn't surprising of course. After all, as the philosopher Gaston Bachelard wrote, 'our house is our corner of the world ... our first universe.'[*]

At the heart of children's construction work is the power of imaginative play. As children build and construct, the flow of pretend play helps shape what they make. They use their constructions to stand for things as they play out what they know and understand about their world. An adult may ask: *What are you making?* But for the young child exploring one idea after another, it can be more important to build something that remains in a state of *becoming*.

Materials such as blocks, boxes, scrap cardboard and timber off cuts – even upturned furniture and plastic milk crates – provide a host of opportunities for improvising and constructing things. They invite thinking about structure and balance. Whether children build child-high towers or small enclosures to creep into, or make paper aeroplanes, they are face to face with something tangible, something that physically exists in the same space as they do. This is the appeal of making sculpture.

In a captivating book about architecture, architects Donlyn Lyndon and Charles W. Moore give us an insight into children's structures. By creating structures around themselves, the authors write, 'Children claim ... a world their own size, magnifying their presence in the larger world where they generally don't quite fit.'[**]

Wooden blocks are among the most marvellous materials we can give children. Their geometric beauty inspires them to build with precision and an eye for pattern.

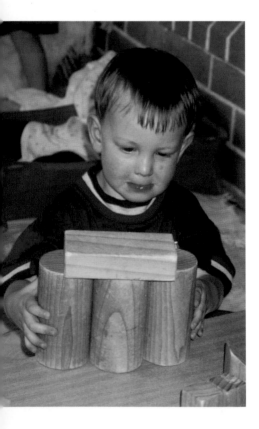

[*] Gaston Bachelard, *The Poetics of Space*, tr. Maria Jolos, Beacon Press, Boston, Mass., 1969, p. 4
[**]Donlyn Lyndon and Charles W. Moore, *Chambers for a Memory Palace*, The MIT Press, Cambridge, Mass., 1994, p. 141

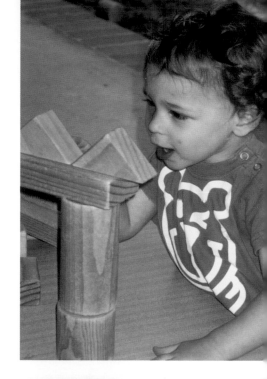

To stack blocks one on top of the other is a great thrill. It helps having a low table to work on.

APPRECIATING WHAT CHILDREN DO

Among children's earliest building materials are toy blocks. Toddlers learn about blocks by carrying them around from place to place. Often they amass them higgledy piggledy in piles. In time they begin to see them as building material, and attempt to stack blocks one on top of the other.

Because there are many identical shapes in a set of blocks, children can do what they love: repeating the same actions over and over again. As the photographs show, repetition is a key feature in the towers, rows, walls and flooring children make.

Each child has a different building style. Some attempt to straighten edges as they build blocks one on top of the other, carefully judging what they need to do in order to balance them. Others are less interested in achieving stability and more interested in inventing new combinations.

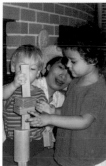

Children may label their structures: *It's a house/a boat/a road*. But as building continues and pretend play evolves, structures may change. Gradually children tackle more difficult structures: for example, bridges, four sided enclosures and stairs. This takes a lot of experimentation.

As children master particular building techniques, they begin to use them in more elaborate structures. For some, rich pattern-making is the main interest, while for others it can be an invented story that unfolds as the block landscape grows in size.

As building partners, children exchange and pool ideas.

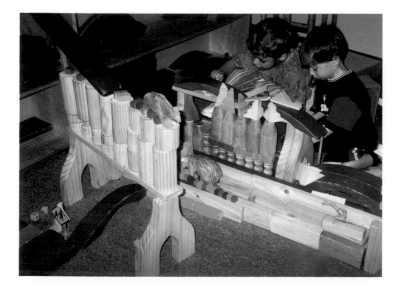

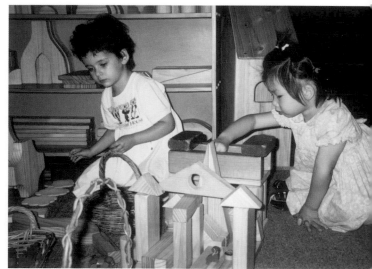

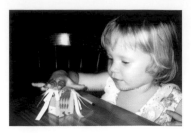

Cardboard construction work depends on children's cutting and pasting skills and their experience with sticky tape. Three-year-olds often begin by taping items together, or stacking and pasting items on top of each other.

Older children may like to create elaborate structures with large items such as grocery boxes. For example, for three six-year-olds the highlight of constructing a tower (three boxes high) was inventing a lift for transporting tiny people from one floor to the next. Made from a small cardboard lid that slid up and down a string, this contraption captivated all who gathered to watch.

Doors, trapdoors and windows feature in many box constructions. To six-year-old Carrick, the most memorable part of transforming a grocery box into a magic castle was making a trapdoor in the roof that opened and shut. The castle remained a treasured object in his bedroom for years.

'Magic Rooms' – a construction by four five-year-olds.

- Your interest in the emerging structures, even if you don't say much, gives support. Take photographs or try making sketches of children's work. This shows that you take it seriously and of course creates a record.

- Invite children's comments: *Can you tell me what's happening here?* Make positive remarks such as: *I see you've stacked these blocks carefully.*

- Offer materials for cardboard construction when children are able to use glue with care (see Materials and Tools overleaf) or are proficient in using sticky tape. Help children develop skills in using these adhesives.

- Help children brainstorm ideas. Try asking: *How can we change this box?*

- If children want to create openings in heavy cardboard, they should draw lines where they want you to cut with a sharp knife. You can cut openings away entirely, or cut a rectangle along three sides and leave the fourth side attached if they want a hinged effect.

- Encourage children to work together by providing a base, such as a large box or board, for two or three to work on. Try to anticipate special requirements as their work develops. For example, if it seems cardboard 'chimneys' may require 'smoke', you could search for materials like fluffs of cotton wool, filmy strips of gauze, wisps of wool, or curly wood shavings.

FURTHER CHALLENGES

Paper construction The first step in creating the scenes in the photograph was to make the characters. Children drew figures on firm paper, cut them out, and then made them stand up by using a strip of card folded at right angles and pasted to the back of each figure. This was not as straightforward as it may seem. Children had to plan ahead to make a figure drawing *wide enough* to accommodate the supporting strip. Some had to modify their usual way of drawing figures and make several versions before their figures would stand.

The next challenge was to create the forest and street scenes. The children wanted to make trees, buildings and doorways taller than the characters. This meant they had to measure, estimate, and think about the proportions of objects in relation to each other. So although they were creating fantasy scenes, they were also observing and recording aspects of the real world.

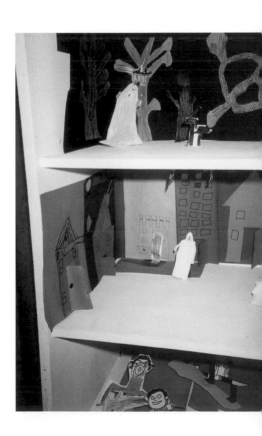

'Storyland' scenes arranged in a classroom bookcase by five- and six-year-olds.

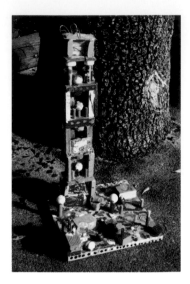

A painted tower by four- and five-year-olds is made from wood offcuts glued together.

Wood construction Children can create wooden sculptures by gluing offcuts of softwood with non-toxic PVA glue.

Dioramas A diorama is a scene with three-dimensional objects. It can be built up on a board or in a large box. Let dioramas develop from children's ideas. For instance, when four children had made dinosaurs out of clay, four-year-old James piped up: 'Hey! I know! Let's make a dinosaur park!' The other three children immediately understood what he meant. All I had to do was to give them a board and help them find some props.

A sheet of cardboard can become a street, a field, a river, or the open sea. Young children like to play with their dioramas and will keep on adding details to suit stories as these unfold.

'Dinosaur Park' offers great scope for play as children arrange and rearrange items. In the middle is a piece of clay with 'dinosaur foot prints'.

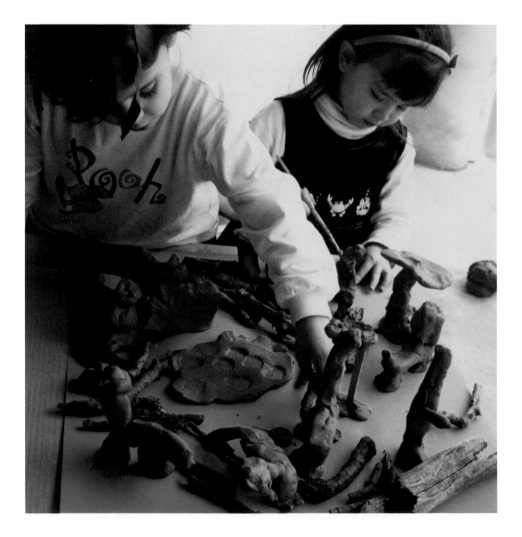

Give children ample time to gather materials and build, as well as pack away. If possible, allow buildings and constructions to remain in place over days.

Block builders need a protected space, away from general traffic in a room, so that pieces are not accidentally knocked over. A mat on the floor or a low platform is a suitable base. When not in use, blocks need to be stored in an orderly fashion so that they are ready for use again.

Cardboard and paper construction works best on a table, which should be covered with a sheet of plastic or paper. Alternatively, use a sheet of heavy cardboard or masonite as a base. Organise tools and adhesives, together with materials and props in shallow containers, on another table or nearby shelf.

MATERIALS AND TOOLS

Block construction A good set of wooden blocks in units of different sizes and shapes and in sufficient quantities is not cheap, but it is an investment that lasts years. Children can also combine blocks from more than one set. Plastic modular blocks offer excellent building opportunities too.

Accessories Offer experienced children some of the following: tiny wooden or plastic animals, figures and vehicles, shells, corks, cotton reels, narrow lengths of perspex, balsa wood, tiny fabric pieces, lengths of ribbon, small carpet pieces, seed pods and buttons. Items must be large enough to stop them being swallowed. Provide them in separate containers so that children can choose easily.

Cardboard and wood construction Look for materials such as containers, cardboard cylinders, egg cartons and offcuts of wood. Sort them according to shape and size so that they look like building materials and not a pile of scrap.

Firm grocery boxes offer many possibilities. Remove torn or unwanted flaps. Occasionally you might have children pre-paint boxes with black or white acrylic paint to cover any lettering and provide a contrasting background.

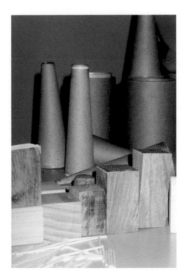

For creating details Offer some of the following: light card pieces, corrugated card, coloured and metallic paper, wallpaper, fabrics, pieces of carpeting, cellophane, acetate, short pieces of dowelling, balsa pieces, tiny boxes, film canisters, egg carton segments, cotton reels, corks, plastic mesh.

For making 'people' Provide materials such as pipe cleaners, paddle-pop sticks, dowelling pieces, corks, pieces of wood, fabrics, wool, tiny boxes, heavy paper, light card.

Dioramas For boards, use sheets of heavy cardboard, perspex offcuts, plywood or masonite. To make the board look interesting, cover the surface with black or coloured paper, corrugated card, cloth, felt, etc. Children can then arrange objects and props on the surface. As they begin to play a story often develops, and this can suggest further things to make. If children are not too impatient to assemble their scene, they might first paint the surface with acrylic or tempera paint. Wide brushes (from a hardware store), rollers or sponge pieces dipped into paint in a saucer or lid will enable them to cover surfaces quickly. Alternatively, they might paste collage materials onto the surface to create roads, rivers, etc.

Adhesives Sticky tape, non-toxic PVA woodworking glue. Have paper towels nearby for wiping sticky hands. Use a damp sponge to wipe away excess glue.

Tools Scissors with rounded ends (make sure they cut), hole punch, stapler, paste brushes (or paddle-pop sticks). Felt-tip pens, pencils, rulers. Short-handled paint brushes (optional).

Paints (optional) Acrylic or tempera paints (see under Painting, page 60).

SEE ALSO
Discovering Forms **21**
Claywork **66**
Collage **76**
Puppet People **99**

Printmaking

Children discover printmaking by themselves. Chance fingerprints, footprints on the beach or in snow, prints from muddy boots – these interest children and arouse curiosity.

The next step is to make prints with paint and simple objects such as geometric shapes of wood or firm foam.

What excites printmakers into making print after print? A seductive mixture of physical action, expectation and surprise. It's the feel of hand actions – holding and dabbing and pressing – and the excitement of not knowing what the object in your hand may actually produce. It's the delicious moment of anticipation as you lift the object from the printing surface. And then the *surprise*: a print that's hardly ever quite as you expected.

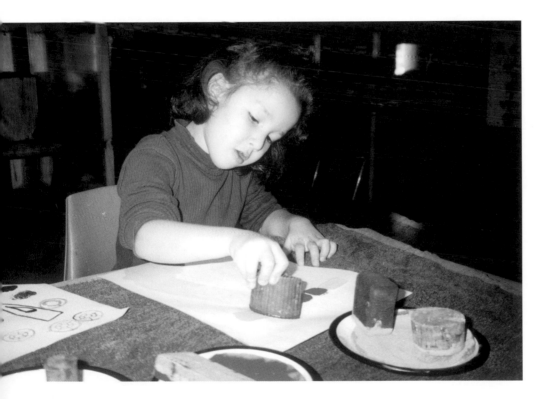

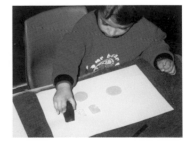

A print lets you see shapes in an extraordinary way.

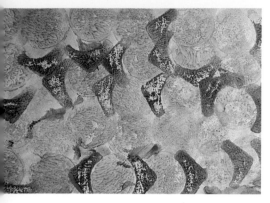 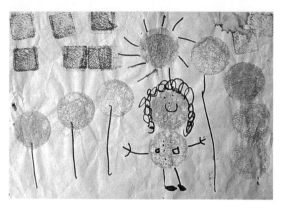

The left-hand example shows an all-over pattern, while this one shows a combination of drawing and painting.

APPRECIATING WHAT CHILDREN DO

When children begin printing, they concentrate on mastering the actions involved, and so tend to print randomly. They delight in repeating actions to investigate cause and effect.

As their skills develop, children begin to organise, arrange and combine their shapes. For example, they might print objects in rows or around the edge of the paper.

Depending on the shapes available, children may combine them – for instance, placing small shapes within bigger ones. Ideas for making figures, animals or objects may emerge as they spot unexpected combinations.

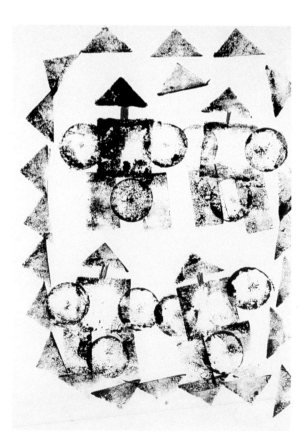

Pattern made by a girl (4 years 6 months) by using pieces of firm foam and acrylic paint at an easel. She began by printing in the top left section of the sheet a combination of five shapes that made a symmetrical configuration (a figure perhaps). She repeated this motif three more times and then printed the surrounding border.

- Begin with only a few simple objects and colours.

- Rather than demonstrating to children what they should do, invite them to show you how carefully they can *dab, dab, dab* the object on a paint pad so that it's well coated with paint. Then ask them to show you how they can press the object firmly on a piece of paper without moving it around.

- In my experience, the more I ask children to show me how carefully they can perform an action, the more they become conscious of technique and the care and skills needed. As a result, *they* gain control over a medium instead of being controlled by it. And in showing you how well they can do certain things, they also learn how to teach skills to each other.

- Remind children to take time and work slowly. Comment on their arrangements; for example, *You've put little circles inside your big circle.*

- Take care that working conditions remain inviting: replace objects if they're smothered in paint, replenish paint pads, and ensure that each child has clean colours and a clean working space.

- Comment on children's discoveries when they find different ways of making a print. For example, some may try overprinting (printing one colour on top of another). Or they might use objects in different ways; for example, rolling a cotton reel across paper.

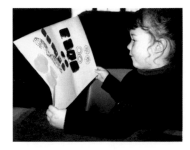

Overheard at the printing table: 'Yellow-yellow! Red-red! Black-black! Green-green!' This four-year-old spontaneously 'reads' aloud her arrangement of printed colours.

FURTHER CHALLENGES

There are many different printmaking methods, and almost anything will make some sort of print. But not all methods offer young children the same scope for invention. My advice is to avoid techniques that rely too much on adult involvement or are merely novel for novelty's sake. If you stick to simple objects that make clear prints and let children add details with pen or crayon, in time they are likely to surprise you with designs, patterns and pictures.

Vary printmaking experiences by printing on black or dark-coloured surfaces with white or pastel colours (make pastels by adding white to colours). Try printing in shades of one colour – for example, a range of greens.

TIME AND SPACE FOR PRINTMAKING

Try to offer printmaking regularly as it takes time to develop printing skills.

Set up a printmaking area with table and chairs. Young children concentrate more readily when sitting rather than standing. Arrange materials so that steps in the process flow easily. Make a drying space for wet prints so that the printing table remains uncluttered.

Object printing This simple method (also called block printing) offers great scope for image-making. It consists of pressing an object coated with paint onto a surface.

Objects Start with geometric shapes (e.g. pieces of wood or firm foam) that are easy to hold and produce bold prints.

Small toy blocks from building sets are ideal shapes to print with. If surfaces are very glossy and don't 'take' paint, use sandpaper to roughen them. Other objects include circular lids, short lengths of dowelling, corks, cardboard cylinders, cotton reels and hair rollers.

Paints Use one of the following: non-toxic acrylic paint, tempera, or paste made with cornflour (cornstarch) and food dye. Also try food dye without paste, or non-toxic water-based printing ink. Each type of paint produces a different result. Test the paint to make sure that it produces good prints.

Paint pad Place a thin sponge pad or folded paper towelling in a shallow dish. Brush paint onto this, making sure that it soaks in well.

Printing area Cover the printing table with a blanket or towel or layers of newspaper, and put a plastic cloth over the top. This surface makes for better prints, but make sure that it's even. Children can also print at an easel, but as this presents a hard surface, offer blocks of firm foam for printing rather than wooden ones.

Paper or cloth Use absorbent (non-glossy) paper or cloth for printing. You may need to experiment with a few surfaces at first.

Leaf printing Use flat leaves with prominent veins. Apply paint sparingly to the *underside* of the leaf with a piece of sponge or a brush. Then place a piece of paper on top of the painted side and rub gently. Alternatively, place the leaf on paper, painted side down, with another sheet on top and rub gently.

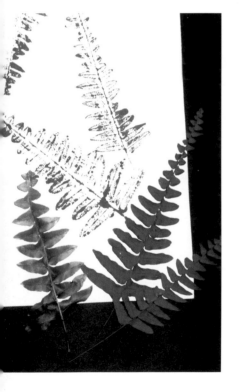

A leaf print shows a delicate tracery of veins.

SEE ALSO
Discovering Shapes **18**
Discovering Colours **26**
Discovering Textures **31**
Discovering Patterns **33**

Rubbings

Place a sheet of paper over the underside of a leaf, rub over it with crayon, and what do you see? An impression, a *rubbing*, showing the leaf's shape and tracery of veins.

You can use this technique on many surfaces, and it works best when done with loving care. Rubbings offer a wonderful way to see details in everyday things that are often overlooked.

Older children are more likely to persist than younger children (and obtain results that delight them) because rubbing needs a steady hand.

INTERACTING AND GUIDING

- Show children how to hold the crayon on its side and how to keep the paper steady. Encourage them to hold the paper for each other.

- Help children obtain results that show details clearly. (Rubbings done in a hurry and with paper that is too thick usually disappoint.) Tell children that making rubbings takes a little practice and encourage them to make several.

Making rubbings: a chance to marvel at details and patterns.

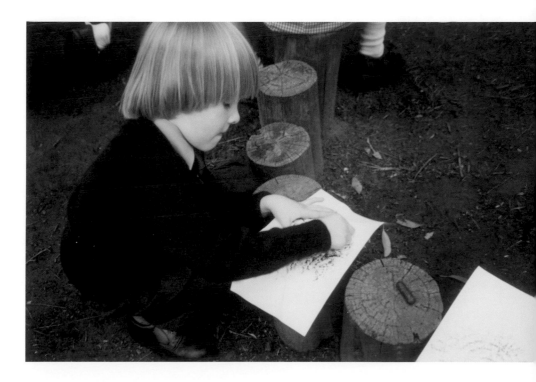

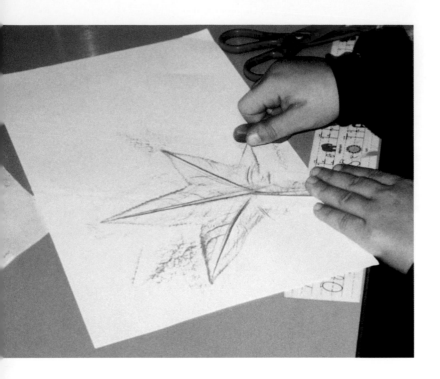

METHOD AND MATERIALS

Surfaces Find surfaces that are reasonably flat so that paper will not tear when rubbed. Try leaves, keys, coins, tree rings in a cut log, certain kinds of bark, weathered pieces of wood, floor boards, brick walls and tyres.

Paper Use lightweight paper, such as lightweight bond. Firm paper tends to give poor results, while newsprint often tears.

To make a rubbing Place paper over a textured surface. Rub slowly and firmly over the paper with the broad side of an unwrapped wax crayon or oil pastel. Dark colours generally produce more effective rubbings on white paper than light colours. Older children may also try using compressed charcoal or soft (6B) pencils. Vary the pressure according to the texture of the surface. The paper must not move.

Wax resist To make light-coloured crayon rubbings stand out, children can brush over them with a soft brush dipped in a contrasting dark wash of food dye dissolved in water.

Cut-outs Children can cut around rubbings and use them in collage, or make books with them.

SEE ALSO
Discovering Shapes **18**
Discovering Texture **31**
Discovering Patterns **33**

Bookmaking

To hold and turn the pages of a self-made book can be enthralling. When children begin to 'explode' into writing (as they often do before they can read), bookmaking has enormous attractions and extends their fascination with letters and numerals.

Bookmaking involves creating a series of drawn, painted or collaged images (with or without writing), and then binding or stapling the sheets together. You can either bind the pages when drawings are complete, or first assemble pages into a book before picture-making begins. Writing can be done by an adult according to a child's dictation, or by a child using either 'pretend' writing or actual words and sentences. Pages can be attached along the left-hand side, bound in the middle, or folded in concertina or zigzag fashion.

Tiny books have a special attraction. The advantage of small pages is that they can be filled quickly and children soon enjoy the rewards of turning their own. I remember my four-year-old son and seven-year-old daughter spending an entire afternoon making a 'library' of miniature picture books, scarcely bigger than large postage stamps. They even created a library system for borrowing and returning the books.

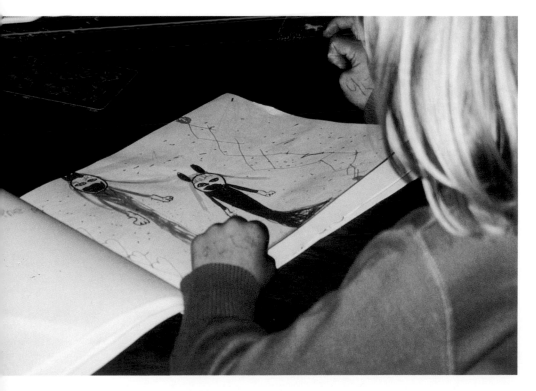

Making books can be an enchanting experience.

- There are various ways of starting bookmaking with children. Sometimes they make a series of drawings that seem to belong together. All they need do with your help is staple them together – and the idea of bookmaking is born. At other times children may discover that a sheet folded in half gives them four 'pages' on which to draw. With your encouragement they can make this into a book.

- Alternatively, give children blank pages already assembled into variously shaped books. Pages can be stapled or stitched together. They can also be tied together: punch holes along the left-hand edges, thread wool or cord through the holes, and tie a knot or bow.

- When children decide to illustrate an event such as a trip to the zoo, help them work out a beginning, middle and an ending to their story.

- Discuss book covers with children: *What are they for? What goes on a cover? How can you decorate a cover?* Suggestions for covers could include collage, painting or printmaking. Try ruling a border to make a frame – children enjoy the challenge of working within boundaries.

MATERIALS AND TOOLS

Paper Small to medium sheets of medium weight white or coloured paper (bond, cartridge or litho paper), light card for cover (optional).

Drawing media Fine felt-tip pens, oil pastels, crayons, coloured pencils, lead pencils.

Tools and adhesives Scissors, stapler or hole-punch, paper paste, sticky tape.

Binding (alternatives to staples) Use wool or cord for threading pages, or needle and thread for stitching them.

Optional Collage materials such as coloured paper, photographs, rubbings and favourite stickers.

SEE ALSO
Discovering Shapes **18**
Drawing **42**
Collage **76**
Printmaking **91**

Puppet People

'Hey! Wings to fly! He's flying!' Utter surprise and delight cross Joel's face. A strip of tissue paper suddenly flutters from a paddle-pop stick in his hand. It's an amazing moment for this child of barely three years. Within an instant, his laboriously taped paper fragment has become a moving creature!

Anything a child can hold and manipulate can become a puppet – a paper scrap, a wooden block, a spoon, a toy. Often before they're even finished children animate their puppets, making them move, sing, grunt and squeak.

Through role-playing with puppets, children can explore ideas about themselves and their world.

I've called this section 'puppet people' in order to emphasise a fascinating feature of children's work. Even though their puppets are often animals or creatures, they are essentially humans in animal dress. Like Peter Rabbit in the classic story book, who is not really a rabbit, the animals children create usually stand in for humans. 'It's a person dressed *in* a bird,' four-year-old Cam informed me as we looked at his clay sculpture of a bird/person.

Don't expect very young children to put on a show. For them 'performance' means making a puppet pop up within an improvised theatre for only a moment – and then disappear. This can be an exciting experience for a young child. After all 'appearance and disappearance', 'presence and absence' are powerful themes that young children constantly grapple with in their pretend play.

By four or five years of age children may delight in making puppets sing or tell stories before an audience. Experienced children may make more complex productions with scenery and props.

Stick puppets are simple and quick to make.

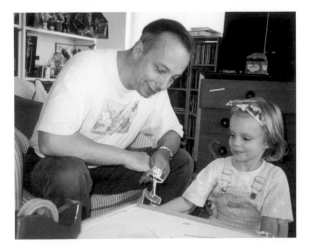

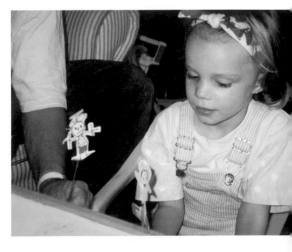

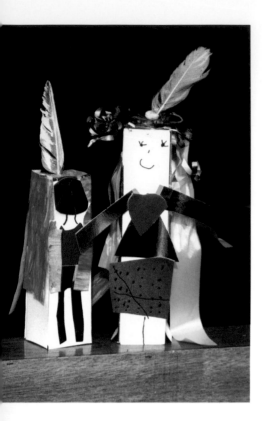

INTERACTING AND GUIDING

- Often the idea of making puppets comes from children's response to materials. The trigger might be an appealing bit of scrap that suggests curly 'hair'. Or it might be a cut-out drawing of a figure or animal. Seize these moments and help children look for additional materials.

- Encourage children to invent their own puppet-making methods, but be ready to give technical assistance. Joining methods using glue or sticky tape usually need an extra hand. (Sticky tape achieves a quicker result for impatient three-year-olds; older children are better able to wait for glue to dry.)

- Ask children about the characters they're making – what clothes do the puppets need? How do they move? What do their voices sound like?

- Clear a space for a performance to take place before an impromptu audience. Puppeteers can stand behind a child-height bookshelf or a table turned on its side, draped with cloth. Alternatively, make a theatre out of a large box. Children can also animate cut-outs on an overhead projector or against a shadow screen.

METHODS, MATERIALS AND TOOLS

While there are many ways of making puppets, the following basic methods give children scope to improvise and invent their own creatures.

Stick puppet Attach a cut-out drawing (on firm paper or light card) to a stick with sticky tape. Use a paddle-pop stick, thick balsa wood strip or thin piece of dowelling. Stick puppets can also be used as shadow puppets.

Finger puppet To the back of a cut-out drawing attach a semi-circle of paper to fit the finger like a ring.

Three-dimensional puppet Any three-dimensional object such as a small cardboard container, cylinder, block of wood or wooden spoon can be transformed into a puppet by pasting on drawn features such as eyes and mouth, and attaching 'clothing'.

You will need firm paper (e.g. cartridge), light card, felt-tip pens, coloured pencils, crayons, scissors, sticky tape, paper paste and paddle-pop sticks or pieces of dowelling. Perhaps add oddments such as tiny pieces of coloured paper, fabric and wool. For gluing non-paper items use non-toxic PVA glue.

It's a good idea to sort materials into categories. For example:

Heads/bodies Cardboard cylinders, pieces of wood, small narrow rectangular boxes (e.g. from toothpaste, photographic film), egg carton segments, paper cups, corks, matchboxes, cotton reels.

Hair Wools, yarns, unravelled carpet wool, curly wood shavings, raw wool, fur, furry fabric, steel wool.

Clothes Small pieces of fabric (plain, patterned, shiny – pinked edges add appeal), leather scraps, lace, net, braids, etc.

Limbs Pipe cleaners, drinking straws, paddle-pop sticks. Note that the lack of arms on a puppet frequently doesn't matter to young children.

SEE ALSO
Discovering Light and Shadow **37**

Indonesian shadow puppet. Cut-out figures are the basis of the shadow puppets of Indonesia, and also of China, Turkey and Greece – to name just a few other countries with a tradition of using shadow puppets. The puppets are held by a rod or wire against a translucent screen and lit from behind. Traditionally they were made from brightly coloured parchment or hide specially treated to make the surface translucent.

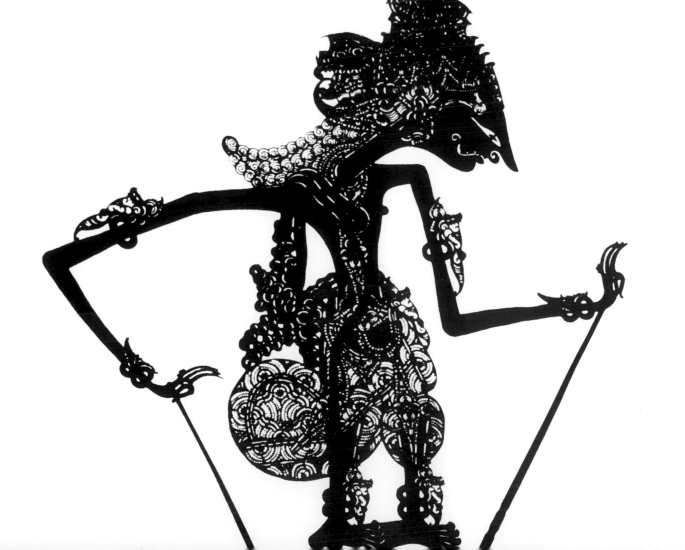

Sharing Interests and Passions

Remarkable things happen when children share and investigate ideas about a topic over days, weeks, and even months.

In this chapter are some examples of what can take place. They show how different media, such as drawing and claywork, influence what children do. By making various kinds of images around a topic, children can reach new understandings of whatever it is that interests them.

Topics often pop up quite unexpectedly – as in the story told opposite.

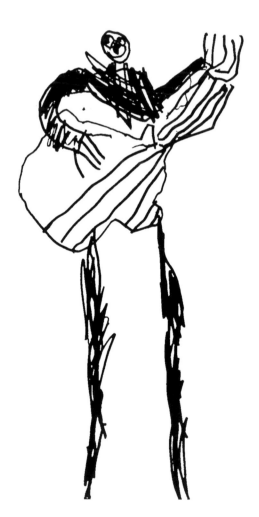

Tails Straight and Wiggly

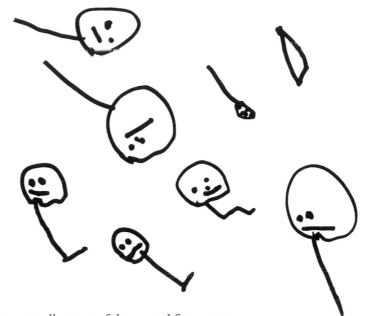

Each day on arrival in a day care playroom, a small group of three- and four-year-old friends have been spending time watching and talking about recently hatched tadpoles. One morning one of them suddenly exclaims: 'Look at the tails! They're wiggly and curly when they move, but when they're not moving they're straight!'

Responding to this interesting observation, the teacher suggests the children draw tadpoles and also make some out of clay. Being used to exploring ideas in this way, the children eagerly start drawing. While making tails, both straight and wiggly, proves far from easy, they are so fascinated they persist for days. Each makes several versions.

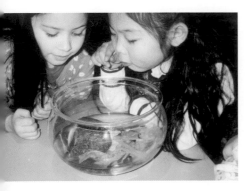 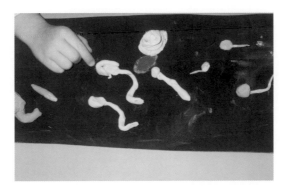

'Tadpoles', felt tip pen drawing and clay work, by girl (3 years 8 months). It's interesting to see how each material has its own 'voice'. While both the drawing and claywork show contrasting tails, in this instance it is clay that enables the child to express the very essence of 'wiggliness'.

Castles: Enclosures for the Imagination

This example describes a small group of four-year-olds (again a group of friends) working both side by side and in partnerships. Their passion centred on making castles, and it lasted several weeks. It all began with a chance conversation.

Jeff: Kings live up high in the clouds. They also live in a castle.

Julie: A princess lives in the garden under the ground.

Effie: A queen lives in a golden castle.

Jason: Fairies and princesses could live in a tree but a king lives in a castle.

Clearly castles – and who lives in them – are a topic of great interest to these children. Although they have diverse views on *who* lives in a castle, they all agree, as their teacher discovers, that castles are gold in colour.

HOW DO YOU DRAW CASTLES?

The children decide to draw castles but are unsure how to start. They soon find that in order to draw the characteristic castle shapes they have in mind, they have to refer to pictures. A hunt for good pictures ensues.

The children draw various individual versions of castles – a mix of the remembered (from pictures) and the imagined.

Picture books, an encyclopedia and postcards offer exciting images that inform, jog the memory or fire the imagination. Without these resources it would be difficult for the children to achieve the complexity in their drawings that they do.

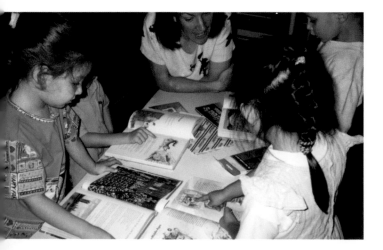
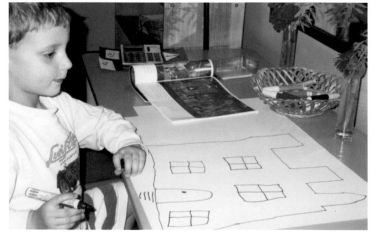

The children discuss a cut-out version of a castle.

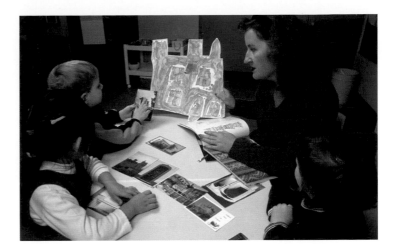

A THREE-DIMENSIONAL CASTLE

A new development: the children decide to make a castle out of blocks. Working together on a common goal isn't easy. However, having developed a shared understanding of castles over several days, they are able to collaborate and exchange ideas.

The children begin to build a castle with blocks. It will not be dismantled at the end of the day, but kept on a board so that work can continue.

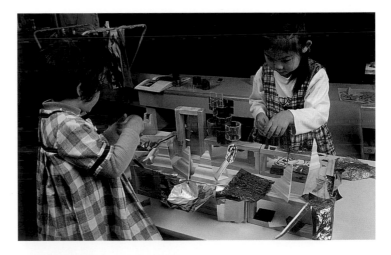

The children make paper people to live in the castle. Shiny collage materials add a touch of magic.

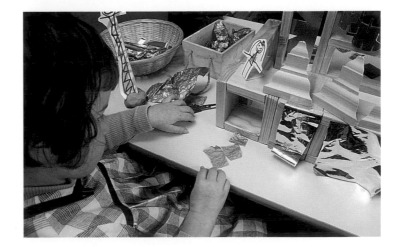

A new challenge: the children make
drawings of the block castle.

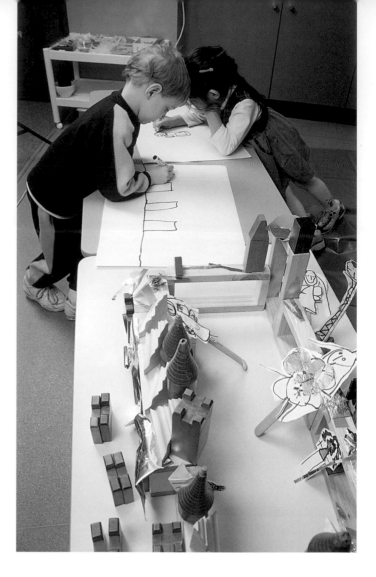

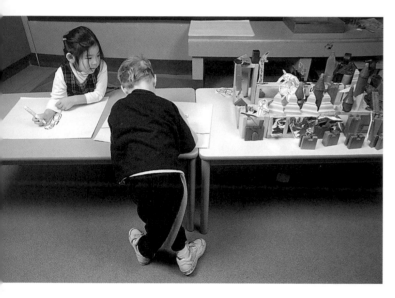

It's not hard to see why castle-making kept this small group fascinated for weeks. After all, as architects Donlyn Lyndon and Charles W. Moore have noted, the ramparts of a castle 'make a powerful enclosure for the imagination, the finite centre that lies at the top of the heart of most fairy tales.'[*]

[*] Donlyn Lyndon and Charles W. Moore, *Chambers for a Memory Palace*, The MIT Press, Cambridge, Mass., 1994, p. 84

The World of Trees

'Trees' is a rich topic that can inspire and enchant. A slow stroll among trees can be the beginning of a journey of discovery.

Give children a challenge: how many new things can they see? When armed with clipboards, paper and pens or pencils for drawing, children may look at familiar trees in a new light.

They can make a myriad discoveries as they run hands along trunks, feel the texture of bark, and find oozing sap, ant trails and grooves left by insect larvae. They can finger age-rings on sawn ends of branches, peer into tree hollows, smell foliage and gather fallen leaves and bark.

They can speculate on why a tree has bark or theorise on how trees obtain water. They can ponder on the interior life of a tree and imagine what life underground might be like.

Here is a good example of how drawing can be a wonderful learning tool, a process of investigation.

How large is a tree trunk? Children measure the girth of a tree.

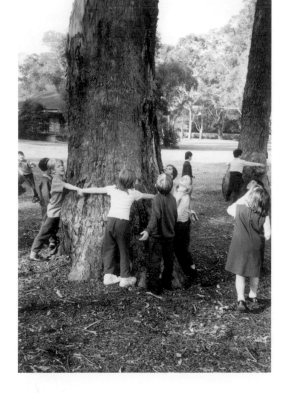

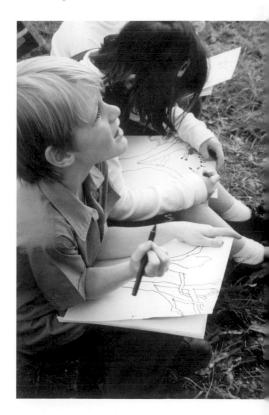

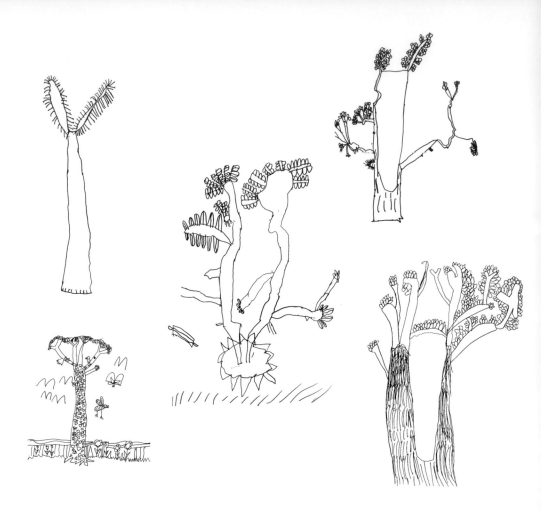

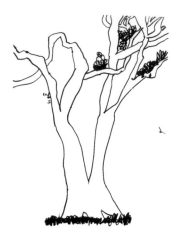

Drawings based on observation. The images show a blend of the observed, remembered and the imagined.

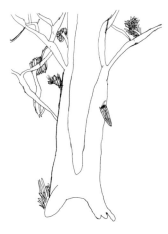

GREEN BLOOD

On the first day after a walk among trees, five- and six-year-olds discussed what they had seen, drawn and found. Here are some of their comments about their drawings:

Amy: I like leaves. Some leaves are old and some are new. Some leaves have holes in them. Some are from different trees.

Rina: When leaves fall down they won't survive. Then the tree will be sad. Some leaves are a dark colour.

Omar: Bark is on the outside, it's like skin.

Janey: Some trees have blood.

Dan: There was some kind of blood called sap coming out of the tree. And there was other ones that didn't have sap.

Jo: Green blood. When it's dead it has brown blood. When it's alive it has green blood.

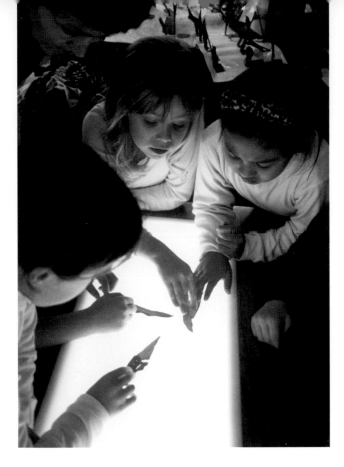

A light table enhances the beauty of leaves and inspires some to make detailed drawings.

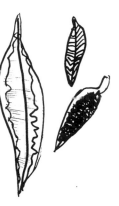

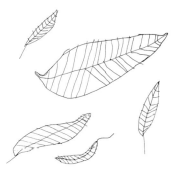

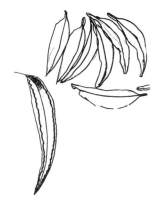

TREE IMAGES

Through further drawings, cut-outs, rubbings and clay sculptures, the children extend ideas over a period of five weeks for about an hour a week.

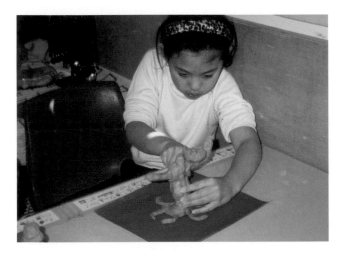

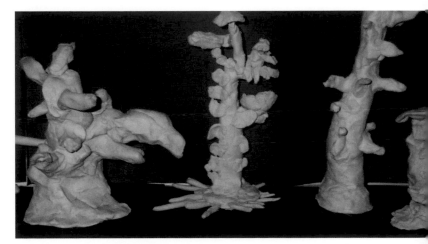

Having made several drawings of trees, the children are able to make complex tree sculptures.

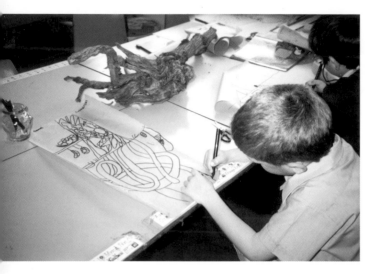

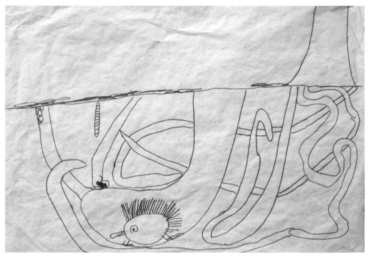

A hidden world: ideas about life in the soil under a tree. Children seem intuitively to understand trees as mini-ecosystems connected to animal life – as well as to earth, sky, sun, wind and rain.

HIDDEN WORLDS: WHAT MIGHT BE UNDER TREES?

Brimming with excitement after making clay trees, some children turn their minds to ideas about life underground and make other drawings.

Steve: I drew an underground place. Animals live in it and a caterpillar lives in it.

Leslie: Next to the roots are some ant homes. They have walkways to their homes. I wanted to make the homes a bit away from each other.

Ray: Some roots are above the ground and some roots are under the ground. There's a sand frog and there's a rabbit. They all have separate burrows.

As children listen to each other's ideas and see each other's work, they have opportunities to learn that there are different points of view. Through exploring a topic in different ways and from different perspectives, they expand their understandings.

As this poem shows, there is more than one way to view a tree.

TREE

bird home
leaf home
ant home
lizard home
twig
    branch
         caterpillar
             butterfly
   home

seed shade
sheep shade
cow shade
horse shade
wallaby shade
people shade
ground shade
sun shade

a tree is a green umbrella
with brown bits

JENNY BOULT

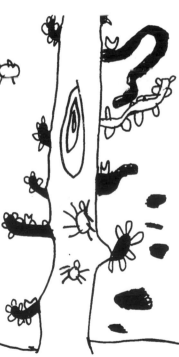

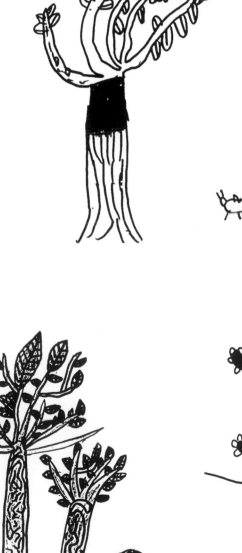

Journeys with Children

My stories about tadpoles, castles and trees offer mere glimpses into what is possible. Depending on their interests and what else is happening around them, children can extend their explorations much further. There are many paths they can follow. The important thing for adults is to be fellow explorers. Be prepared for the unexpected. Don't feel that you have to arrive at a specific point – enjoy the journey.

Some points to keep in mind:

- Whether topics arise from children's conversations and discoveries, or whether you choose them, they must be significant to children. Find out what they already know about a topic.

- It's often a good idea to begin with drawing before offering other materials. This allows children to channel their thoughts in an uninterrupted flow from mind to paper. When their minds teem with images, experienced image-makers are often bursting to represent their ideas. They may want to make five or six drawings one after the other. Others may take longer to begin and prefer to see what others do first (a sensible way of learning).

- Don't expect all children to be simultaneously interested in the same topic or the same aspects of a topic.

- Help children share their expertise in pairs or trios. This can be a good way to develop a spirit of collaboration. Give them time to develop and exchange ideas about a topic over days, weeks, or even months.

- Collect reference material and resources for children to choose from: picture books, encyclopedias, photographs, postcards, plastic models and found objects.

- As work progresses, encourage children to recall and reflect on what they've discovered so far. Let them discuss photographs of their experiences.

- The key to knowing how to extend children's thinking lies in several sources: your observations and interpretations of their experiences, records of their conversations and photographs, as well as the images they themselves create. Questions that arise are vital because they spark investigation. How do you draw wiggly tails? What's under trees? Questions are central to creative work.

For further guidance and inspiration, see titles listed under 'The Reggio experience', page 131-2.

SEE ALSO
Drawing from Observation **48**
Murals, Banners and Hangings **56**
Claywork **66**
Rubbings **95**

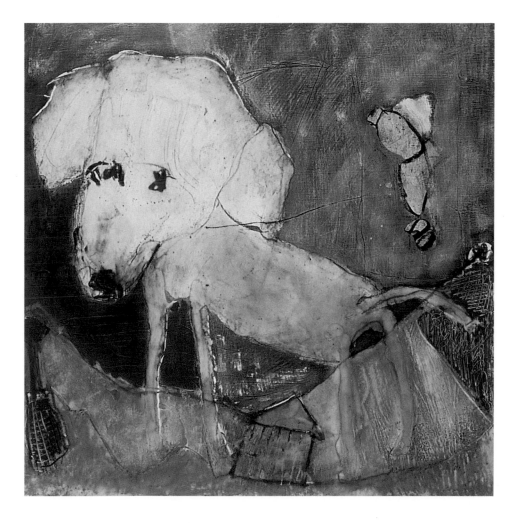

The eyes of this little dog hold our attention. Yearning for something yet waiting patiently, she stares with a loving gaze, quietly accepting human foibles. Like Geoff Harvey's sculpture of dogs (see page 121), this painting does not set out to create an illusion of reality. It draws us into empathising with an animal's feelings.

Audrey Rhoda (Australian)
Song For Samantha, 2000
Wax on board, 50 x 50 cm

Courtesy of the artist

Other Matters

Children's surroundings – and everything that happens in them – affect how children think and act. This chapter raises matters that may shape their experiences with materials. It includes the use of studio spaces and practices such as documenting children's experiences. Also included is the use of colouring-in books – about which I'm often asked – as well as questions such as *Should I draw for my child?* and *What about gallery visits?*

Creating Studio Spaces

A special space for creating images benefits young children greatly. Why?

Whether it's a corner in your home, in a day care or preschool playroom or a school classroom, a special space supports children because they get to know 'what happens here'. It is much easier for young children to develop skills in a familiar situation. It's also much handier. A special space that functions like a studio/laboratory/workshop enables children to extend and share ideas in imaginative yet skillful ways.

A studio space need not be indoors. Let me describe an example. It is a small area on a verandah in a day care centre, a pocket of space that seems to encircle children in a welcoming embrace. At its centre is a clay table.

This table is only ever used for claywork, and is never moved. It is both separate from all else on the busy verandah, and also a part. When an adult sits at this table, it draws children like a magnet. It's not unusual for them to spend more than an hour in this space, often days in a row. As the set-up doesn't change from day to day, they know what to expect. It is a space where everyone sees claywork as serious business. Materials and tools are close at hand in a cupboard accessible to children, and a nearby display of claywork reminds them of earlier ideas.

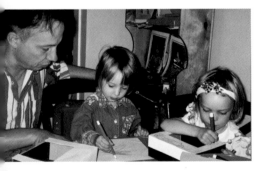

A corner of the kitchen table can be a good place for drawing and making things.

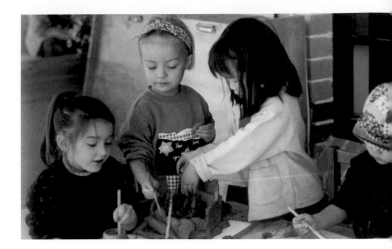

A space where seriousness and playfulness intermingle: a spot on a verandah devoted to claywork. This photograph of 'Rapunzel's Supermarket' in the making shows the spirit of imaginative perseverance that I believe a special studio space can inspire.

Some points to keep in mind:

- Choose a sheltered well-lit area (or areas) away from general traffic in a room. If working with numbers of children, think about creating an inviting place that entices them to gather in small groups, yet is equally conducive to working alone. The 'look and feel' of a studio space influences children. Let your imagination and creativity come into play when designing a space – think of creating one where you would like to be too.

- If it's not possible to leave materials permanently in one spot, try to set up experiences regularly in the same place. Certainty and predictability are important for young children.

- Adequate table space for each child is essential. Provide chairs as children can work for longer periods when sitting.

- Offer basic materials of the best quality you can afford. Make sure materials give satisfying visual 'feedback' and that tools are in good working order. Arrange attractive containers of materials and place them invitingly on shelves accessible to children. For children at home, have materials available in stackable baskets, boxes, plastic containers or purpose-made tool boxes.

- Choice of materials is important, but too much choice can at first be overwhelming. Creativity often thrives on constraints. A limited range need not be a drawback as long as children can use the materials in open-ended ways.

- Display found treasures and have on hand magnifying glasses and resource material like picture books and an encyclopedia. Add pictures and photographs to spark imagination – or induce moments of reverie.

- Adult supervision is essential whenever young children use materials and tools. Arrange furniture and equipment with safety in mind. Read the labels to ensure materials are non-toxic, and check that items cannot be swallowed and have no sharp edges.

Displaying and Documenting Children's Work

It may not always be easy to find room to display children's work or time to do so; however, do try to display a few examples at a time. When you display children's work, it shows that you value their efforts. Displays remind them of what they've done and can inspire further ideas. They can add beauty and interest to studio spaces. But they can also be fairly pointless.

The sadness of seeing rows of similar images comes back to me as I recall visiting with my daughter Karin, then seven years old, an exhibition of children's art work at her school. As she gazed up at the myriad of almost identical paper butterflies festooned across the walls, her face fell. Half angrily, half despairingly, she sighed, 'Well, I think one of those is mine, but I don't know which.' How sad, I thought: staff had generously given of their free time to create a display – but of what? To what purpose? 'Art' was being used here as a public relations exercise. Children and the potential wealth of their ideas and imagination were overlooked.

There are ways of creating displays that can do justice to children's lively minds. When a display reveals something of the thinking, making and sharing of ideas that went into the work, it tells a story. This is why it is so valuable that you take notes of ongoing experiences by small groups of children and write comments on them. When you put up some of the comments together with photographs of the children at work and transcripts of their dialogues, it adds great interest to displays. It helps you and the children recall experiences and so inspires further work, and it informs families about the program.

When done well, documentation gives us a window into children's thinking and learning. It can show how children bounce off each other's ideas. In doing so, it reveals not only the interactions of a specific group, but sheds light on young children's thinking in general.

However, when documentation is to be displayed, choose your material carefully. Always be mindful of the need to protect confidentiality. Documentation on display should never reveal personal details. Nor should it encourage readers to compare children. It is important that staff and families all understand the purposes for displaying documentation. From the children's point of view, having an adult document what they do and say – provided it is with their consent and participation – is a positive experience. It tells them their thoughts and actions are important.

In addition to displaying work, store a selection of children's work (dated) in portfolios. These can consist of folders (either made from sheets of card or purchased) or plastic A3 sleeves. You will find material on documentation and the use of studios in titles listed under 'The Reggio experience', page 131-2.

Should I Draw for My Child?

While I love drawing – and many children know that I do – I don't draw for them. When children ask you to draw a particular object, it's usually because they lack confidence in their own ability to draw it. Although it's tempting to draw on request, I caution against it. Why?

Young children don't approach drawing the way adults do. They use a different 'system'. When children ask me to draw a dog, say, I have no idea what sort of image they want. If I draw a dog in an adult fashion, they can't use this information to make their own drawings (although they may find watching me entertaining). If I draw in a simple cartoon-like manner, I'd be giving them a formula. This is likely to set them up for failure because it's difficult to remember a formula invented by another. And a formula does not help children *teach themselves to draw*.

As already mentioned, 'I don't know how to draw it' often means 'I don't know how to start'. Talking things through with children can be a great help (see Andrew's Bird, page 44). Older children benefit from opportunities to draw objects in front of them. For instance, when Jake had difficulties drawing a bicycle from memory, we set up a bicycle in front of him (see Drawing from Observation, page 48).

While talking things through with children takes time, it is well worth it. Your reward? Seeing their immense pride and joy when they realise they have taught themselves another drawing strategy, mastered another step in exploring and representing their world.

Colouring-in Books

Colouring-in books: should we buy them? Here is my view.

Most colouring-in books are a bit like junk food – harmless in moderation but definitely not recommended for a regular diet. Why? Because they don't assist children in 'learning to see' or draw. They may keep hands busy but they rarely provide food for the imagination.

That said, it's true that many children like colouring-in books, and for short periods seem to find the task of colouring-in a calming experience. Particularly for a child sick in bed, the repetitive actions as well as the chance to handle bright colours may even be therapeutic.

It is sad, however, when programs provide children with pre-drawn colouring-in activities in the belief that these are 'educational'. Some claim that learning to colour within outlines helps children develop fine-muscle control, and so assists them in gaining 'pre-writing' skills. That may be so, but why give children *pre-drawn* outlines to fill in?

When children are pleased with their own drawings, they usually take great care in colouring them. Pride in their drawings comes from the confidence of knowing that they *can* draw. And confidence comes from having had many opportunities to draw. If colouring-in activities are offered too frequently, children miss opportunities to learn to draw. Less confident children may even lose faith in their drawing abilities.

Copying

Should you be concerned if children copy images? It may surprise some people that virtually all artists at some stage or other copy images in order to learn. Young children often begin a drawing by 'borrowing' elements they see in the drawing of an admired peer. 'Borrowing' can be one of the most important factors influencing how children learn to draw.

Copying has a long history. Before the modern era, apprentice craftspeople were expected to imitate their masters' techniques. This tradition still continues today – for example, in the teaching of traditional Chinese calligraphy and watercolour painting.

I remember copying an illustrator's technique at the age of about ten because I wanted to learn how to draw shininess. I wanted to create an illusion of silk but didn't have a clue how to convey the vision of loveliness I desired. So when I came across a watercolour illustration of a silken-sashed fairy, I set about copying it in pencil. I found I could create a silky appearance by leaving tiny white spaces as I coloured the sash – the white spaces suggesting light bouncing off the surface.

Adults sometimes misunderstand children's purposes in copying. An artist friend recalls an incident in her childhood when her mother, seeing her copy parts of an illustration, remarked critically: 'You're not copying are you?' According to my friend, 'This was actually quite shattering. I remember thinking, but why? – I'm learning from this – what's the problem? To me it was natural, but to her it was something I shouldn't be doing.'

Both my friend and I had copied work that we admired in order to understand how to do something. Generally it seems that children can only copy shapes they already know how to make, or are on the verge of knowing how to do. They actually 'copy' very little – only bits that help them do whatever it is they want to do.

Sometimes, however, children copy images because they have no confidence in their drawing abilities. This is when it's important to find ways of restoring their confidence. You might suggest they try a different medium – such as clay or collage – where they may have no notions about how 'good' or 'bad' they are.

Despite the benefits of selective copying, it is not something that adults should introduce to young children. Children are the best judges of knowing when and what to copy in order to learn how to draw. It makes no sense for them to copy something without understanding why or to what purpose. This can only lead to frustration.

What about Gallery Visits?

Seeing works of art first-hand in a special place can be an enchanting experience for young children. When sculptor Geoff Harvey's pack of lifesize dogs was on display in a public gallery, it immediately caught the eye of many a child visitor.

The key to having an enjoyable experience with children in a gallery or art museum is to be well-prepared, enthusiastic about the exhibits, and ready to participate in children's experiences.

Try to find out about an exhibition ahead of time. Identify a few works of potential interest to children, and perhaps collect relevant postcards and photographs. Talk to children about the exhibits before you go. If taking a large number of children, plan to divide them into *small* groups, each with an adult solely responsible for that group.

Once at the gallery, expect young children with their unquenchable curiosity to be intrigued by everything, including escalators, uniformed attendants and washrooms! You may need to explain to them why they should not touch exhibits.

When looking at a work of art, invite responses and questions from the children. What do they notice? What do they think the artist was thinking about? Why do they think the artist used these materials/colours? Talk about works of art in ways that relate to children's own experiences.

After a visit, give children opportunities to relive their experience. For instance, after a visit to an exhibition of sculpture, teachers gave preschoolers large sheets of paper and charcoal for drawing. To their surprise, the children made drawings of a kind they had never done before. The following day the teachers placed some borrowed sculpture equipment on a mat for the children to play with. Two three-year-olds immediately got to work with this, inventing an imaginative scenario. Remarked Ben to Keiran: 'We're sculpture people, aren't we?'

You will find suggestions for planning gallery and museum visits among the titles listed on page 131. Contact education officers at galleries and museums for information about programs for young children, as well as outreach services and travelling exhibitions to communities in remote areas.

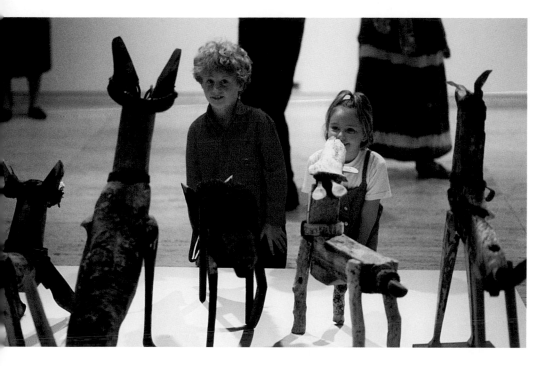

Made from old brooms,
brushes, a bicycle seat,
weathered table legs and
other bits and pieces,
these dogs are the essence
of alertness and doggish
energy. Each has its own
character, each asks
to be seen face to face.

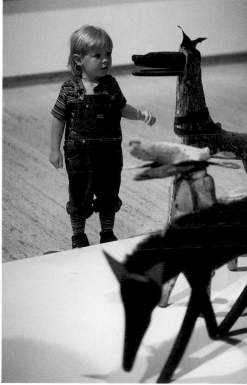

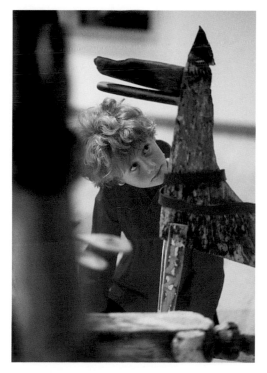

Geoff Harvey (Australian)
The Pack, 1997-98
Mixed media, varied dimensions

Courtesy of the artist, Robin Gibson
Galleries and Art Gallery of
New South Wales, Sydney

Sunlight and Shadow

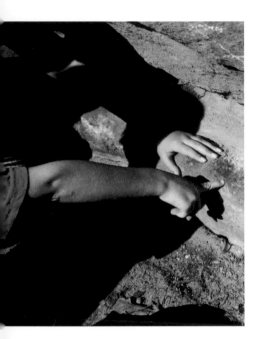

Our journey is drawing to a close. Before it ends, however, there are some further thoughts and ideas I'd like to put forward. They are presented under the four headings used in the previous pages. To remind us of what's covered under these headings, I've borrowed that wonderful device that A. A. Milne used to describe the contents of each chapter in his *Winnie the Pooh* books, namely, the words 'in which'. A delightful example is 'Chapter IV *In Which* It Is Shown That Tiggers Don't Climb Trees' (Milne's italics). I hope readers will uncover other '*in whiches*' here to ponder and discuss.

MAGIC IN EVERYDAY THINGS

In which we pay attention to looking at the world with children and note their sensitivities to lines, shapes, forms, colours, textures, patterns, light and shadow.

Underlying the text and photographs on pages 11–40 is a focus on children's relationships with others and their world of objects, materials and natural phenomena. Here I want to re-emphasise the significance of children's *dialogues* with materials and the natural world. Why 'dialogues'? To many adults, a dialogue with, say, a piece of paper is not an easy idea to come to grips with. As a teacher laughingly admitted at a workshop, 'As adults we're so used to imposing our will on materials and thinking in terms of stereotyped things we've been taught (like making paper lanterns) that I'm finding it hard just to let a piece of paper "speak" to me'. So true! And yet it's what children do spontaneously. This is how they (like adult artists) discover the *potential* in materials.

How might you respond to toddlers' play with materials? Give them time to explore a few basic materials – without the need to *make* something 'because it's time to do art'. Notice what they notice. Watch how they pick up ideas from each other. (For an inspirational account and analysis of what can happen when adults pay serious attention to children's play with materials, see Vecchi and Giudici (eds) under 'The Reggio experience' in Further Reading.)

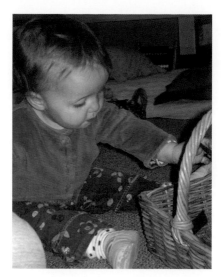 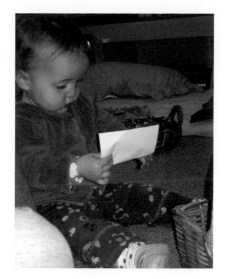 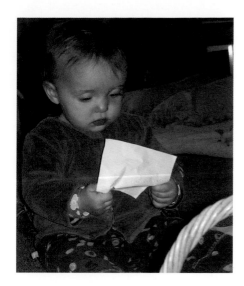

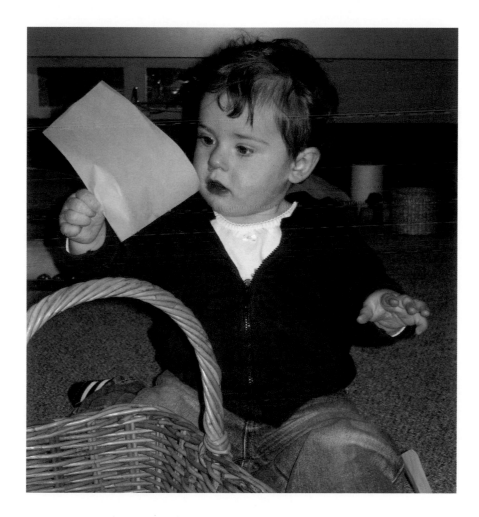

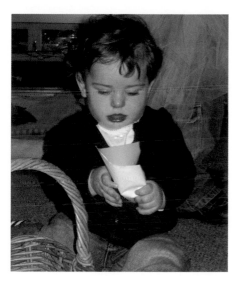

Smooth one moment, crumpled the next, a sheet of paper is full of surprises! Finding out about materials – the look and feel of them, what they can and cannot do, and how they can *change* – is not only essential to learning about the world, it's also essential to the process of learning to make visual images.

Wonder in grains of sand. On a suburban footpath some neighbourhood children and I stopped to look at a spill of pinkish red and gold from a sandstone outcrop. Sorting the sand according to colours proved irresistible.

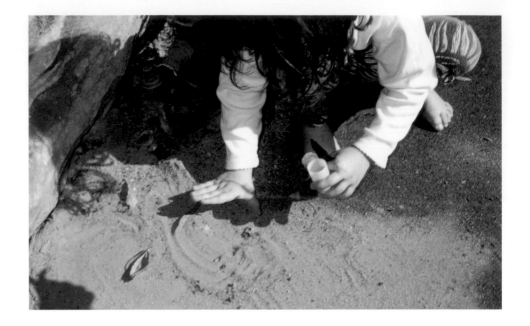

The photograph above serves as a poignant reminder to me that a sense of connectedness with the earth needs to start early. In our world of diminishing resources, overabundance of material goods, and often over-cloistered children, it seems to convey a timely message. Of course, developing environmental awareness has long been a goal in early education. Here I simply repeat my plea: let's make environmental awareness an integral part of children's art experiences.

Feeling the spikiness of dry leaves and listening to their rustling: a small moment that could be an everyday one, yet sadly often isn't. We need to create many opportunities for children to find their place in the natural world.

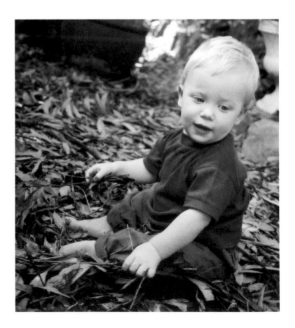

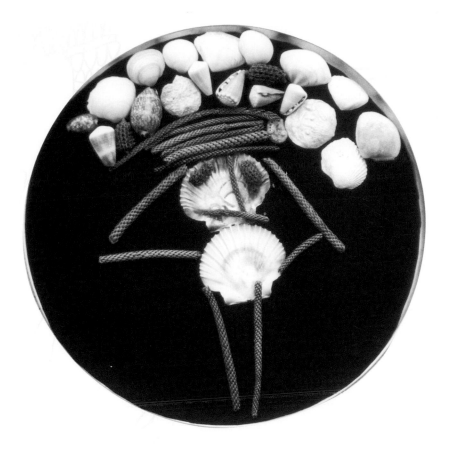

Shells and dry Norfolk Island Pine leaves (needles) arranged on felt without glue by a girl (4 years 8 months). Imagination and creativity flourish when children have time to choose, and build relationships with, objects that intrigue them.

As part of a commitment to promoting care and respect for the natural world, centres have long used found and recycled materials (such as egg cartons), though often in predictable and conventional ways. However many programs today, rather than simply regarding these materials as alternatives to purchased art materials for collage and construction, are re-evaluating them as rich resources to be used for their own sake. Wood, fabric, fibre, foil, cardboard, plastic, old metal, new metal – these are the stuff of a child's everyday world. Each has intrinsic qualities worth investigating. Finding out which materials can curl, bend or flutter and dance in the air – or which lend themselves to investigations into the play of reflected light, for instance – can be both magical and thought provoking. The potential in materials to fire the imagination is vast. (See AGAC *et al*, Curtis and Carter, Gandini *et al* (eds), Topal and Gandini, and Vecchi and Giudici (eds) under 'The Reggio experience' in Further Reading.)

In which we look at ways children explore ideas through drawing, painting, claywork, collage and construction.

Pages 41–101 can only hint at some of the complexities of children's image-making. I urge you to observe how *variously* children use drawing, painting and other media. Notice how their intentions and purposes may differ – an aspect overlooked in earlier theories of children's graphic development. For instance, rather than making pictures about how things *look*, children may use lines and shapes to represent sound and movement, or make representations that function like maps or diagrams of 'what might be'. (Page 46, for example, has a drawing about *Star Wars* that represents actions and events in time.) Drawings reflecting mediated images from popular culture are also common. And as television images of world disasters proliferate, these too are reflected in children's work – particularly when children have opportunities to talk about what they've seen.

Increasingly, educators urge that we acknowledge the darker side of life as it impacts directly, or indirectly via the media, on children's lives. How to assist children to deal with issues related to social justice, or disturbing or tragic events, is a question that many ask. (See titles under 'Facing hard questions' in Further Reading.) Here I can only emphasise that we need to give children every opportunity to use visual language (drawing, painting, claywork and so on) in ways that allow them to give voice to thoughts that they may be expressing – but we're not hearing.

SHARING INTERESTS AND PASSIONS

In which we look at children's collaborative investigations.

Pages 102–13 offer glimpses into the exciting cycle of inquiry that can begin when children work together. The social dimension in children's artwork – how they share and bounce off each other's ideas, not only about topics of interest but also, importantly, how to solve graphic problems – is an aspect I've explored in *It's Not a Bird Yet: The Drama of Drawing*. In this book, however, my purpose is to introduce the idea of collaborative investigations, both long-term and short. For rich accounts of what is possible, see titles under 'The Reggio experience' in Further Reading.

OTHER MATTERS

In which we touch on matters that affect children's artwork: studio spaces, display, documentation, adults drawing for children, colouring-in books, copying, and gallery visits.

Here I want to add another 'matter': the importance of teachers and families *exchanging* ideas and information about children's artwork. Why? From what I hear, families and teachers are not always on the same wavelength when it comes to children's artwork. That's hardly surprising – in any community there will be competing and conflicting views about 'art' and, therefore, also about 'children's art'. In trying to find some common ground between differing views of children's work, it might be helpful not to use the word 'art' at all.

Let's instead find effective ways to explain that the focus is on children's thinking and how they use drawing, painting, claywork and so on as a *visual language* to explore and communicate ideas. Ways to illustrate this may include displays (or booklets) with photos, examples of work and comments by children together with captions aimed at broadening awareness of the many different ways children learn; or presenting PowerPoint presentations or video clips of children in action (with permission from families, of course).

However, if teachers also ask families to shed light on aspects of children's work, then there can be a true exchange of information and a meeting of minds. When this happens, everyone benefits and learns – as in the following example.

It takes place in a day care playroom where I've placed a coffee-table-sized book about the art of modernist Spanish artist, Joan Miro, for children to browse through – or ignore. Simon (just three, a child who rarely draws and paints) looks at it.

'Matians! Matians!' he exclaims, jabbing his finger on a painting in the book. Most viewers would see the painting as being content-free; it shows a horizontal row of irregular-sized black blobs and a sweeping vertical stroke in red on a blue background*. But Simon is rapt. Dismissing other paintings, he repeatedly returns to this one. I am mystified. Later, however, fellow teacher Janet Robertson is able to ascertain, by showing tiny plastic animals to Simon, that 'matians' refers to Dalmatians. Good. But why is he so excited? Janet learns from Simon's mother that he adores the video, *101 Dalmatians,* and his favourite image is one in which Dalmatians appear to streak across the screen like a sea of dots. The significance of this dawns on me as I watch Simon unexpectedly make a painting of three large circular shapes in a row beside a vertical line. He then finds his favourite Miro painting and, comparing it with his, says with satisfaction, 'The same!' Over the ensuing days he makes several representations of Dalmatians: he has found a visual language that *he* can use, and that we can now all appreciate.

Which is my point. It was not until the adults exchanged observations that anyone was able to appreciate Simon's breakthrough – that he had seen something in Miro's painting that not only connected with his passion for Dalmatians, but significantly contained imagery that he could use *to suit his own intentions or purposes.* (I won't assume to know what these might be, but we can guess they're to do with his feelings for Dalmatians.) I think this anecdote reveals something very interesting about how children learn to invent and use visual language to make sense of their experiences.

It showed me again that the more teachers and families can exchange information, the deeper our understanding grows of why children do what they do. And we then become more able to appreciate and explain to others how deeply resourceful and competent young children can be.

* Joan Miro, *Blue II,* 1961, which can be found on the internet by typing the artist's name and the title into a search engine. The book Simon looked at contained both abstract and figurative paintings.

Recipes

Paste

Blend three heaped tablespoons of cornflour (cornstarch) to make a thick cream.
Add $1^{1}/_{2}$ cups of boiling water, stirring all the time.
Mixture should form a thick paste. Add more water if necessary.
(It will thicken as it cools.)

Paste Paint (1)

Make paste as above, but add more water until the mixture is clear
and suitable to use with a brush.
Add a few grains of food dye and stir with a brush. Test the colour
on a piece of paper and add more dye if necessary. Allow to cool.

Food dyes (edible vegetable dyes) yield brilliant colours. You need only
buy red, blue, and yellow, as these mix to make purple, orange and green. Dyes in
powder form are available from art suppliers and good toy stores. You can also use
liquid dye from supermarkets, but these colours are weaker in strength.

Paste Paint (2)

Blend 12 level tablespoons of cornflour (cornstarch) with one cup of
cold water and add sufficient boiling water to the whole to make a litre.
Boil for one minute until clear and thick. Add dye as per recipe 1. Allow to cool.

Finger paint

In a large saucepan mix $^{1}/_{2}$ cup cornflour (cornstarch) with $^{1}/_{2}$ cup of cold water.
Add 1 cup boiling water.
Bring to boil on the stove.
Remove from heat when thick and clear. Add a few grains or drops of food dye or a
teaspoon of non-toxic powder paint. Stir well. Allow to cool.

Play dough

2 cups plain flour
$^{1}/_{2}$ to 1 cup of cooking salt
1 cup cream of tartar
2 tablespoons cooking oil
2 cups boiling water
A few grains powdered food dye or drops of liquid food dye

Mix dry ingredients, then add oil. Add dye to water and mix slowly with dry
ingredients. Knead the mixture as it cools. If it is very sticky add a bit more flour and
cream of tartar, but be careful not to add too much. (The mixture loses stickiness as it
cools.) If stored in an airtight container, the dough will keep a week.

Further Reading

The titles are grouped under headings for convenience.

The Reggio experience/Reggio-inspired practice

Reggio Emilia is a small town in northern Italy where a remarkable educational project has developed over 50 years and is continuing to evolve in more than 30 infant-toddler centres and preschools. Internationally acclaimed for their quality, these public services are inspiring educators around the world. I warmly acknowledge the influence of the Reggio Emilia experience in reinforcing, deepening and challenging my understanding of early learning. The breathtaking beauty of the Reggio environments for children continues to excite my imagination and shape my thinking. Nevertheless, the material presented in this book does not attempt to imitate what has become known as 'the Reggio approach'. The Reggio experience cannot be imitated. But it can inspire others to explore their own ways of enabling children to realise their potential as knowledge-builders and image-makers. What you see in this book are Australian examples from places and communities where adults aim to offer children experiences not only rich and engaging, but also provocative and challenging.

AGAC, Friends of Reggio Children Association, Municipal Infant-toddler Centers & Preschools of Reggio Emilia, *Remida Day*, Reggio Children, Reggio Emilia, Italy, 2004.

Cadwell, Louise Boyd, *Bringing Reggio Emilia Home: An Innovative Approach to Early Childhood Education*, Teachers College Press, New York, 1997.

Cadwell, Louise Boyd, *Bringing Learning to Life: The Reggio Approach to Early Childhood Education*, Teachers College Press, New York, 2003.

Curtis, Deb, and Carter, Margie, *Designs for Living and Learning: Transforming Early Childhood Environments*, Redleaf Press, St.Paul, MN, 2003.

Edwards, Carolyn, Gandini, Lella & Forman, George (eds), *The Hundred Languages of Children: The Reggio Emilia Approach – Advanced Reflections*, 2nd edn, Ablex, Greenwich, Conn., 1998.

Fu, Victoria R., Stremmel, Andrew J., Hill, Lynn T. (eds), *Teaching and Learning: Collaborative Exploration of the Reggio Emilia Approach*, Merrill Prentice Hall, Columbus, Ohio, 2002.

Gandini, Lella, Hill, Lynn, Cadwell, Louise & Schwall, Charles, *In the Spirit of the Studio: Learning from the Atelier of Reggio Emilia*, Teachers College Press, New York, 2005.

Giudici, Claudia, Rinaldi, Carlina & Krechevski, Mara (eds), *Making Learning Visible: Children as Individual and Group Learners*, Project Zero, Cambridge MA/ Reggio Children, Reggio Emilia, Italy, 2001.

Katz, Lilian G. & Cesarone, Bernhard (eds), *Reflections on the Reggio Emilia Approach*, ERIC Clearinghouse on Elementary and Early Childhood Education, Urbana, Il., 1994.

Malaguzzi, Loris, *The Hundred Languages of Children*, exhibition catalogue, Reggio Children, Reggio Emilia, Italy, 1996.

Millikan, Jan, *Reflections: Reggio Emilia Principles Within Australian Contexts*, Pademelon Press, Castle Hill, NSW, 2003.

Reggio Children, *Everything Has a Shadow Except Ants*, Reggio Children, Reggio Emilia, Italy, 1990.

Topal, Cathy Weisman & Gandini, Lella, *Beautiful Stuff! Learning with Found Materials*, Davis Publications Worcester, Mass., 1999.

Tarr, Patricia, 'Aesthetic codes in early childhood classrooms: What art educators can learn from Reggio Emilia', *Art Education*, 54 (3): 33-39, 2001. Also online, viewed September 2006, <www.designshare.com/Research/Tarr/Aesthetic_Codes_1.htm>.

Vecchi, Vea & Giudici, Claudia (eds), *Children, Art, Artists: The Expressive Languages of Children, the Artistic Language of Alberto Burri*, Reggio Children, Reggio Emilia, Italy 2004.

Art experiences with children

Adams, Eileen, *Start drawing!* Power Drawing, London, 2002.

Derham, Frances, *Art for the Child under Seven*, 7th edn, Australian Early Childhood Association, Canberra, 2001.

Kolbe, Ursula, *Clay and Young Children: More than Making Pots*, Australian Early Childhood Association, Canberra, 1997.

Kolbe, Ursula & Smyth, Jane, *Drawing and Painting with Under Threes*, Australian Early Childhood Association, Canberra, 2000.

Matthews, John, *Helping Children To Draw and Paint in Early Childhood: Children and Visual Representation*, Hodder & Stoughton, London, 1994.

Pahl, Kate, *Transformations: Children's Meaning Making in a Nursery*, Trentham Books, Stoke-on-Trent, 1999.

Silberstein Storffer, Muriel, with Jones, Mablen, *Doing Art Together*, Abrams, New York, 1996.

Smith, Dee & Goldhaber, Jeanne, *Poking, Pinching and Pretending: Documenting Toddlers' Exploration with Clay*, Redleaf Press, St. Paul, MN, 2004,

Smith, Nancy R., *Experience and Art: Teaching Children To Paint*, 2nd edn, Teachers College Press, Columbia University, New York, 1993.

Topal, Cathy Weisman, *Children, Clay and Sculpture*, Davis Publications, Worcester, Mass., 1983.

Wright, Susan (ed), *Children, Meaning-Making and the Arts*, Pearson, Sydney, 2003.

Development in drawing and painting

Anning, Angela, & Rink, Kathy, *Making Sense of Children's Drawings*, Open University, Maidenhead, Berkshire, 2004.

Arnheim, Rudolf, *Art and Visual Perception: A Psychology of the Creative Eye – The New Version*, University of California Press, Berkeley, 1974. (See chapter 'Growth')

Brooks, Margaret, 'Drawing: the social construction of knowledge', *Australian Journal of Early Childhood*, Vol. 292, June 2004.

Brooks, Margaret, 'Drawing, Thinking, Meaning', TRACEY – Contemporary Drawing Research, viewed 24 June 2005,
<http:www.lboro.ac.uk/departments/ac/tracey/thin/brooks.html>.

Golomb, Clare, *The Child's Creation of a Pictorial World*, University of California Press, Los Angeles, 1992.

Golomb, Clare, *Young Children's Sculpture and Drawing: A Study in Representational Development*, Harvard University Press, Cambridge, Mass., 1974.

Goodnow, Jacqueline, *Children's Drawing*, Fontana Open Books, London, 1977.

Kindler, Anna M. and Darras, B., 'A map of artistic development', in A.M. Kindler (ed.), *Child Development in Art*, National Arts Foundation, Reston, Virginia, 1997.

Kolbe, Ursula, *It's Not a Bird Yet: The Drama of Drawing*, Peppinot Press, Byron Bay, NSW, 2005.

Kolbe, Ursula, 'Seeing beyond marks and forms: appreciating children's visual thinking', in Wendy Schiller (ed.), *Thinking through the Arts*, Harwood Academic Publishers, Sydney, 2000.

Lange-Kuttner, Christiane & Thomas, Glyn V. (eds), *Drawing and Looking: Theoretical Approaches to Pictorial Representation in Children*, Harvester Wheatsheaf, London, 1995.

Matthews, John, *Drawing and Painting: Children and Visual Representation*, 2nd edn, Paul Chapman Publishing, London, 2003.

Robertson, Janet, 'Drawing: making thinking visible', in Wendy Schiller (ed.), *Thinking through the Arts*, Harwood Academic Publishers, Sydney, 2000.

Trevarthan, Colwyn, 'Mother and baby: seeing artfully eye to eye', in Richard Gregory, John Harris, Priscilla Heard & David Rose (eds), *The Artful Eye*, Oxford University Press, Oxford, 1995.

Willats, John, *Making Sense of Children's Drawings*, L. Erlbaum Associates, Mahwah, N.J., 2005.

On art, architecture, aesthetics, imagination and enchantment

This eclectic mix of titles inspired me while writing this book.

Arnheim, Rudolf, *The Split and the Structure: Twenty-Eight Essays*, University of California Press, Berkeley, 1996.

Bachelard, Gaston, *The Poetics of Space*, tr. Maria Jolos, Beacon Press, Boston, Mass., 1969

Dissanayake, Ellen, *Homo Aestheticus: Where Art Comes From and Why*, University of Washington Press, Seattle, 1992.

Isaacs, Jennifer, *Spirit Country: Contemporary Australian Aboriginal Art*, Hardie Grant Books, Melbourne, 1999.

Greene, Maxine, 'Art worlds in schools', in Peter Abbs (ed.), *The Symbolic Order*, Falmer Press, London, 1989.

Gombrich, Ernst H., *The Sense of Order: A Study in the Psychology of Decorative Art*, Phaidon Press, London, 1984.

Hockney, David, *That's the Way I See It*, Thames & Hudson, London, 1993.

Kepes, Gyorgy, *Language of Vision*, Dover Publications, New York, 1995.

Lyndon, Donlyn & Moore, Charles W., *Chambers for a Memory Palace*, MIT Press, Cambridge, Mass., 1994.

Moore, Thomas, *The Re Enchantment of Everyday Life*, Hodder & Stoughton, Sydney, 1996.

Facing hard questions

Fleet, Alma, Patterson, Catherine & Robertson, Janet (eds), *Insights: Behind Early Childhood Pedagogical Documentation*, Pademelon Press, Castle Hill, NSW, 2006.

Greenman, Jim, *What Happened to the World? Helping Children Cope in Turbulent Times*, international edition adapted by Jim Greenman & Anne Stonehouse, Pademelon Press, Castle Hill, NSW, 2002.

Gross, Toni and Clemens, Sydney Gurewitz, 'Painting a tragedy: Young children process the events of September 11', *Young Children*, Vol.57, 3, May 2002. Also available at The Learning Collaborative, 2002, viewed 24 June 2005, <http://thelearningcollaborative.org.paintingatragedy/index.html>.

Vecchi, Vea, 'Poetic languages as a means to counter violence', in Vea Vecchi & Claudia Giudici (eds), *Children, Art, Artists: The Expressive Languages of Children, the Artistic Language of Alberto Burri*, Reggio Children, Reggio Emilia, Italy, 2004.

Acknowledgments
First Edition

So many friends, neighbours and colleagues have encouraged me over three years that it is impossible to thank you individually – my warmest thanks to all. Special thanks to the children and their families for allowing me to take photographs – in my local neighbourhood; at Mia-Mia Child and Family Study Centre, Macquarie University; Kent Road Public School; Birchgrove Public School; Fox Valley Kindergarten; North Shore Temple Emanuel Preschool; Lauriston Girls' School; Bialik College Early Learning Centre and Wesley College, Elsternwick Campus. I am hugely indebted to the welcoming staff, children and families.

For inviting me to visit playrooms and classrooms, my thanks to Robyn Ambler, Deborah Bate, Julie Day, Jennifer Eaton, Daphne Gaddie, Sandy Kay, Sally Jorgenson, Cheryl Israelson, Kirsty Liljegren, Lorraine Lowery, Mary Mauger, Tosca Moseek, Helene Oberman, Joanne Pryce, Sue Ransley, Barbara Raczinski, Janet Robertson, Neil Salvado, Wendy Shepherd and Bronwyn Wheeler. Thanks to Paul Kolbe, Kath Shearer, Jane Smyth, Elena Stevenson and Margaret White for their helpful contributions, and to Jan Millikan, Avis Ridgway and Susan Williams for their valuable assistance.

For kindly granting me permission to reproduce their artwork, I thank Kate Dorrough, Sophie Gralton, Geoff Harvey, Patricia Karbo Jarvis, Edna Mariong Watson, Galuma Maymuru, Audrey Rhoda, Guan Wei and Dhukal Wirrpanda. For facilitating access to artworks, thanks to Errol Davis, Rhonda Davis and Professor Di Yerbury of Macquarie University; Will Stubbs and the Buku Larrnggay Mulka Centre; Dr. Gene Sherman and Penny Betts of Sherman Galleries; Ken Watson and the Art Gallery of New South Wales. For their photography, I thank Jennifer Eaton, Sandy Edwards, Peter Endersbee, Anne Evans and Kirsty Liljegren.

For reading and commenting on the manuscript at various stages, thanks to Margaret Bishop, Philip Bray, Quentin Bryce, John Dunn, Jennifer Eaton, Christine Evered, Eileen Kalucy, Robbie Lawson, Lorraine Lowery, Janet Robertson, Jane St Vincent Welsh, Maggie Videan, Wendy Shepherd, Associate Professor Graeme Sullivan and Associate Professor June Wangmann, and to Christine Stevenson who was my invaluable sounding board on every aspect throughout.

Thanks to Barbara Sherman, Cynthia à Beckett and Jannette Greenwood for their editorial advice and for encouraging me to find my own 'voice', and to Jeremy Steele for his editing and invaluable support. Thanks to designers Kellie Hindmarch and Matthew Robertson for realising text and images into the book I had dreamed of. Lastly, my heartfelt thanks to my daughter, Karin Kolbe – without her vision, dedication and countless contributions, the manuscript would simply never have become this book.

URSULA KOLBE

Index

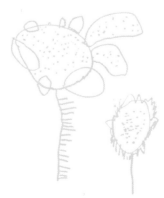

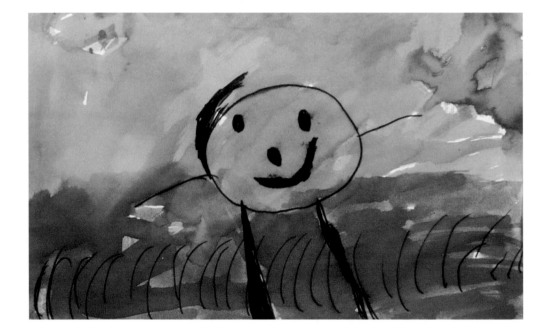